Doing Your Literature Review

Doing Your Literature Review
traditional and systematic techniques

Jill K. Jesson with Lydia Matheson and Fiona M. Lacey

Los Angeles | London | New Delhi
Singapore | Washington DC

First published 2011

SAGE Publications Ltd
I Oliver's Yard
55 City Road
London ECIY IS

SAGE Publications Inc.
2455 Teller Road
Thousand Oaks, California 91320

SAGE Publications India Pvt Ltd
B1/I1 Mohan Cooperative Industrial Area
Mathura Road, New Delhi 110 044
India

SAGE Publications Asia-Pacific Pte Ltd
33 Pekin Street #02-01
Far East Square
Singapore 048763

Library of Congress Control Number: 2010932411

British Library Cataloguing in Publication data

A catalogue record for this book is available from the British Library

ISBN 978-1-84860-153-6
ISBN 978-1-84860-154-3 (pbk)

Typeset by C&M Digitals (P) Ltd, Chennai, India
Printed by CPI Antony Rowe, Chippenham, Wiltshire
Printed on paper from sustainable resources

MIX
Paper from
responsible sources
FSC® C013604

CONTENTS

ABOUT THE AUTHORS

Jill K. Jesson entered higher education as a mature student. She won a First Class Honours BSc in Behavioural Science, and in 1988 was awarded her PhD for a pioneering doctoral thesis on black businesses, both from Aston University. Since then she has worked with multi-disciplinary research teams within the Aston School of Pharmacy, Aston Business School and with M-E-L Research, an independent public services research consultancy. Her publications cover community pharmacy practice, public health and social care. Her special interest in literature review and the idea for this book developed as a result of teaching applied research to pharmacy undergraduates and Business School Masters students.

Lydia Matheson is an Information Specialist working for Library and Information Services at Aston University. She undertook her BA Honours in English at York University and her PG Diploma in Librarianship at the University of Central England. Her current role includes supporting business school students and developing the library's online learning module for staff and students. She is currently Secretary of the Business Librarians Association and a member of CILIP. Before 2002, she worked on Stories from the Web for Birmingham Libraries and the SENCO Electronic Communications Project for the National Council for Educational Technology.

Fiona M. Lacey is a Glasgow native and graduate in Pharmacy, from Strathclyde University. She has been a registered pharmacist since 1982, practicing mainly in community pharmacy. Following a PhD in pharmacology, she gained post doctoral experience of R&D as a laboratory scientist in a UK-based multinational pharmaceutical company. She has been at Aston University since 1997, where she has taught various scientific and professional aspects of Pharmacy to undergraduate and postgraduate students. Her interest in literature review and the systematic review came through years of supervising student research projects. She is currently Associate Dean in the School of Life and Health Sciences at Aston University.

ACKNOWLEDGEMENTS

Several people helped us in compiling this book.

Katie Jesson drew the diagrams in Chapters 5, 6, and 7. Rob Pocock drew the Gantt charts in Chapters 1 and 3, and encouraged us to stick to the project time plan and complete the book.

Thanks to my colleagues Anna Ackfeldt and Nick Lee for their constructive comments on early drafts. Fiona Lacey read through an entire early draft, giving invaluable support and feedback. I am extremely grateful to Mike Luck, who instigated my interest in teaching critical literature review to postgraduate students. He read the manuscript at a draft stage, spotted some spelling errors – the ones that spell-check does not pick up – and offered some advice on readability. I would also like to thank the two anonymous reviewers who gave very candid advice on ways to improve the text. Basia Nowakowska helped with the final formatting.

Patrick Brindle, Anna Coatman and David Hodge from Sage guided and looked after me and the book as it moved through publication.

The following authors and publishers gave permission to use their copyright material.

Open access. Oxford Journals, Oxford University Press, for Hanlon, P. and Carlisle, S. (2008) Do we face a third revolution in human history? If so, how will public health respond? *Journal of Public Health* 30(4): 355–361.

PloS Open Access, for Plos Medicine editors (2006) The impact factor game. *Plos Med* 3(6) e291 www.medicine.plosjournals.org.

Wiley-Blackwell, for Tuch, C. and O'Sullivan, N. (2007) The impact of acquisitions on firm performance: A review of the evidence. *International Journal of Management Reviews* 9(2): 141–170.

Wiley, for the use of Gourlay, S. (2006) Conceptualizing knowledge creation: a critique of Nonaka's theory. *Journal of Management Studies* 43(7): 1415–1436.

Wiley, for the use of Smallbone, T. (2005) How can domestic households become part of the solution to England's recycling problems? *Business Strategy and the Environment* 14: 110–122.

BMJ Publishing Group Ltd, for Lewis, S. and Clarke, M. (2001) Forest plots: trying to see the wood and the trees. *British Medical Journal* 322(7300): 1479–1480, and Sutton, A.J. et al. (2000) Empirical assessment of effect of publication bias on met-analyses *British Medical Journal* 320: 154–157.

National Archives PSI License, for use of Magenta Book GSA (2008) *Government Social Research Civil Service Rapid Evidence Assessment Toolkit*. Available at: www.gsr.gov.uk/professional_guidance/rea_toolkit/index

Cengage Learning, for Jankowitz, A.D. (2005) *Business Research Projects* (4th edn). London: Thompson.

Sage, for Lee, N. and Lings, I. (2008) *Doing Business Research*. London: Sage.

ISI Web of Knowledge, for screen shot Browse facility.

Pharmaceutical Press, for Wilson, K.A. and Jesson, J. (2003) Dispensing activity in a community pharmacy-based repeat dispensing pilot project. *International Journal of Pharmacy Practice* 11: 225–232.

Thompson Learning for Jankowitz, A.D. (2005) *Business Research Projects* (4th edn), London: Thompson.

Wiley-Blackwell for Srivastava, S.K. (2007) Green supply-chain management: a state-of-the-art literature review, *International Journal of Management Reviews* 9(1): 53–80.

Wiley for Curran, C., Burchardt, T., Knapp, M., McDaid, D. and Li, B. (2007) Challenges in multi-disciplinary systematic reviewing: a study on social exclusion and mental health policy, *Social Policy and Administration,* 41(3): 289–312.

Elsevier for Mak, W.S., Poon, C.Y.M., Pun, L.Y.K., Cheung, S.F: (2007) Metaanalysis of stigma and mental health, *Social Science and Medicine.* 65: 245–261.

Aston University for Jesson, J. and Stone, I. (2008) *What do we currently know about barriers to recycling household waste in the UK? a literature review*. Research Working Paper RP 0915. Birmingham: Aston Business School. www.abs.aston.ac.uk or www.m-e-l.co.uk. Accessed July 2009.

BMJ for Smith, K.E., Fooks, G., Collin, J.,Weishaar, H. and Gilomore, A.B. (2010) Is the increasing policy use of impact assessment in Europe likely to undermine efforts to achieve healthy public policy? *Journal of Epidemiological Community Health* 64: 478–487. Online version accessed June 2010.

Open access Biomed Central for Souza, J.P., Pileggi, C., Cecatti, J.G. (2007) Assessment of funnel plot asymmetry and publication bias in reproductive health metaanalyses: an analytical survey, *Reproductive Health* 4/1/3.

Wiley for *International Journal of Management Review* 10(1), March 2008.

Wiley for Turrini, A., Cristofoli, D., Frosini, F. and Nasi, G. (2010) Networking literature about determinants of network effectiveness, *Public Administration,* 88(2): 528–550.

INTRODUCTION

Who is this book for?

This book is intended to be a practical study guide that complements the growing body of guidance on research methodology, and in particular complements the specialised niche of texts on doing a literature review. Since Hart's seminal contribution to 'doing a literature review' in the late 1980s, the methodology of literature review has advanced at a remarkable pace. The take up of the systematic review methodology from biological sciences into other academic disciplines has added considerably to the debate by introducing a more questioning and critical approach to performing a literature review and the manner in which 'traditional reviews' are compiled.

We believe that anyone who has to do a literature review, at whatever level of expertise, will find this book useful. The book is predominantly intended for use by postgraduate students doing their Masters or MBA research dissertation. It should also be of use to anyone studying at PhD level, where it is more likely that a systematic approach to literature to review (or even the use of the systematic review methodology) could be appropriate.

How is this book different?

We assume that our readers have already studied research methodology, or are currently studying on a research methods course. Thus one key point to note is that we do tend to concentrate on the 'know how' dimension. There are many excellent research method textbooks which adequately cover aspects of philosophy of research and the techniques of designing qualitative and quantitative research. This is not to say that research philosophy is not important; students do need to know about research philosophy and about research paradigms, particularly the ways in which research methodology and beliefs have evolved over time, their relative status and importance in different academic disciplines. We do expect you to have a working knowledge of research terminology and methodology, but just in case of difficulties provide a glossary with key concepts to help you.

Our aim is to produce a practical simple guide to meet the needs of a wide range of students. We are conscious that many students want to have easily accessible textbooks, and in particular many postgraduate students are studying and working at the same time, or are distance learners. Some students come to postgraduate studies with a wealth of work experience, but it has been a long time since they were engaged in academic studies and they do need advice on where to begin and how to go about reading articles and making notes before constructing their review. We hope this book will meet that need.

The book is intended to be accessible for researchers from any academic background, so we have borrowed from many disciplines and have chosen from a wide spectrum of topics covering health, environment, business and management fields to illustrate points and techniques. Health and business management subjects tend to predominate because these are the subjects with which we are most familiar; but you do not need to be an expert in any subject to take in the point being made. Topics covered by examples are varied, covering health, pharmacy, finance and business acquisition, supply chain, organisation and management change, and topical environmental issues of recycling. Where possible we use published examples of reviews that illustrate a point being made, the date of publication is less relevant. We acknowledge here the great intellectual debt we owe to the authors whose work we use.

The rationale and history behind the contribution from researchers and from an information specialist

This book has been written by three people from very different backgrounds – social science, pharmaceutical science and library information sciences – thus it has a built-in multidisciplinary approach. We believe that the combination can provide insights that are not always evident in single-subject work.

The social science researcher

Early ideas for this book began when I first started teaching the lecture on 'critical literature review' in Aston Business School in a postgraduate Applied Research Module. I could not recall as an undergraduate or postgraduate student ever being taught anything about reviewing literature. I discovered that many standard research methodology texts did not cover the literature review as a method in itself, although most described the search for information.

Although it is fairly straightforward to teach research methodologies, the part of their research that most students find difficult is writing a critical review of existing knowledge – the traditional literature review. Moreover, we are aware that many students studying for an MSc or MBA who do not have a first degree background in the social sciences have rarely undertaken a research project before. International students sometimes find the need to take a critical approach to literature review as problematic and have to learn how to do it.

The first step in research is to assess what is already known – but until recently this has not been recognised as a research skill in its own right. This skill has to be learnt – the ability to produce 'good' literature reviews does not come naturally. Aside from Hart (1998) there was no text that we could refer students to. This remained the case up until about five years ago when some new texts on the research method of systematic review were published. These books have their own unique selling point and are a complementary source of additional, specialist information for those studying health and social care or education research (listed in Appendix 1). We did write something for our own students (Jesson and Lacey, 2006), but there is still no text covering both traditional literature review and systematic review.

There are still few textbooks that deal specifically with the complete proce-dures involved in what we refer to as a traditional literature review. It is a major contention of this book that researchers have to be able to undertake a traditional literature review as a preparation to moving on to do systematic review. So this book is important for anyone planning to use the systematic review methodology.

A further strong reason for the need for a new generalist textbook is the current focus on the evidence-based movement, which depends on good sys-tematic reviews of current knowledge. So, whether searching for evidence for professional practice, public policy or business management, this is an impor-tant approach to literature review which students should be aware of and be able to do. After undertaking a systematic review myself, I now have it clear in my own mind that we have to be able to do a traditional review – we might call it a scoping review – before we can take on the more concise but comprehensive systematic review.

The library information specialist

In this book we want to show the importance to researchers of the library and information specialists. Inviting a librarian to contribute the literature search chapter in this work is beneficial because of the close relationship between library, knowledge and research. At Aston University, we involve the information specialists in teaching literature search skills to students. This is the contribution made by Lydia Matheson, who is responsible for writing Chapters 2 and 9. Most librarians are skilled researchers: they know how and where to find information. They have experience of searching for resources both in traditional print media and in electronic databases and within what appear to me to be complex internet websites. In universities they often specialise, so whether the subject is business and management or social science or health sciences, they can show you how to do your initial search. The rise of the internet, electronic journals, and access to many public documents has widened the scope and range of information available to the extent that you do not have to go into the library these days to access most of what you want.

The pharmacist researcher

The second contribution comes from Fiona Lacey. Together, we have undertaken several research studies. The contribution from Fiona illustrates the current trend for multidisciplinary collaborative research. Fiona's background is in pre-clinical research and, in addition, she now teaches research methods and supervises Masters-level pharmacy dissertations, an increasing proportion of which are based on systematic review and meta-analysis.

Features of the book

We believe that an important feature of this textbook is its simplicity of language, with the use of 'I' and 'we' instead of the normal academic impersonal passive voice or third-person form, using real-world illustrations and examples from a range of subject areas. The examples are taken from top quality academic journals, from government policy reports and from our own and student works. For readers to get the maximum benefit from examples used we suggest that you look up the original source material. Our intention is that the book will provide an easy introduction to a research task (performing a literature review), which all researchers can relate to with confidence.

One other feature is the importance placed on time management and planning. Chapters 1 and 3 contain a Gantt checklist. Managing your time to meet deadlines is one of the most challenging features in doing applied research. Although there was an original Gantt chart/checklist time plan for this book, there were several unanticipated delays in the writing process. We had not appreciated how long writing a book would take, alongside teaching, marking and doing research, but the time plan on the wall was a constant reminder to get on with it. To effectively manage your time you need to estimate how long each stage/task will take. This book will help you do that.

Layout of the book

As you progress through the book you will move from the basic skills of reading and note-making into the search for information; experienced researchers might want to skim read these sections. In the second part you will learn how to do a traditional literature review before moving on to the more challenging and time-demanding systematic review. Meta-analysis is a specialised synthesis method for advanced reviewers, but here we provide a need-to-know introduction for those interested in the methodology.

Part I provides a general introduction to literature review, to searching, reading, and note-making skills. Part II guides you through the reviewing, synthesis and write-up stages.

Chapter 1 covers definitions: What is a literature review? When would you do a literature review? And which one is appropriate when? Most students are taught to use only highly rated journals, so information on journal rating and peer review issues are discussed in a critical way. Students' ability to use new technology is amazing; nevertheless there is evidence to suggest that their ability to search for and evaluate information on the web is still in question. Some students may over rely on Google, without exploring the wider resources made freely available to them. In Chapter 2 Lydia Matheson provides a technical approach to searching. She introduces the range of resources available through the academic library, covering digital and electronic libraries, and other useful sites. The process of searching is explained step by step. Although the examples are based on Aston University library, the features are likely to be substantially similar in any academic library. Since the electronic provision of material is constantly changing, this work represents a snapshot in time. Chapter 3 focuses on different aspects of reading skills that might help you – how to scan, skim and focus, together with advice on tackling different types of document. Chapter 4 covers the very important topic of writing skills.

Part II presents the detailed steps to produce a traditional review, a systematic review, and a meta-analysis.

Chapter 5 begins the guidance on doing a traditional literature review, and is followed with some suggestions on critical analysis and writing up in Chapter 6. Chapter 7 describes the protocol and procedures necessary to undertake a systematic review. To illustrate points the chapter includes details of a review undertaken specifically for this book. In Chapter 8 Fiona Lacey uses a question-and-answer format to guide you through the basics of the more specialised meta-analysis methodology. Finally, in Chapter 9, Lydia Matheson reminds you of the vital importance of the accurate referencing of material, avoiding the pitfall of plagiarism and falling foul of copyright laws.

If you are a beginner setting out on improving your review skills, work your way through the text to Chapters 5 and 6. If your goal is to undertake a systematic review, you would benefit from reading all the chapters. Whatever your needs, I hope you find the book useful.

PART 1

GETTING INFORMATION

1

PRELIMINARIES

Key Points

- A literature review is a *re-view* of something that has already been written
- A traditional review can vary in format and style
- A systematic review is governed by a prescribed methodology – it is a research method and is used to address a specific research question
- It is possible to work systematically in your literature review, but that does not mean it is a systematic review

---

What is a literature review?

This book is a guide to undertaking a literature review, in which we emphasise that the literature review can be a research method in its own right. We explain that the literature review is a written product; the format varies depending on the purpose of the review. In most instances, the review will be part of a research project and dissertation, but it can be a stand-alone review, one that is not a chapter in a research dissertation or thesis. We are interested in the process of creating a review. Much more attention has been focused on improving the quality of literature reviews, as awareness of the systematic review protocol, with a defined methodology, has raised expectations of what can be achieved by all of us when reviewing literature.

Since the promotion of systematic review as a specialist review in the fields of evidence-based practice, which uses a prescribed, systematic methodological approach, we have an alternative way to review the literature. The systematic review produces an output – for example, a statement of findings to inform policy development – that may not necessarily lead into new research.

The aim of this opening chapter is to present an overview focusing on the context of doing a literature review. We consider some scenarios when you might undertake a review of literature. There is a short discussion of the relationship between a research question and a research project. Literature review is a library or desk-based method involving the secondary analysis of explicit knowledge, so abstract concepts of explicit and tacit knowledge are explored. We critically examine the notion of peer review and challenge the faith placed on the peer review process. The chapter closes with guidance on project planning and time management.

Why do a literature review?

As an academic task the literature review is where you show that you are both aware of and can interpret what is already known and where eventually you will be able to point out the contradictions and gaps in existing knowledge. As with any piece of research, you will have to explain why your review is important, why it is different and what it adds to knowledge. In research, we seek to be original and to make an original contribution to knowledge. In the literature review context that means creating a new dimension or fresh perspective that makes a distinct contribution. There are many reasons for carrying out a literature review, so students should ensure that they are aware of what *they* are being asked to do and ensure that their review does what is required.

Taken as its simplest, traditional form a literature review is a 're-viewing' of the literature. Every student will at some point in their academic career be asked to carry out a review of the literature, usually as part of completing a research project. Sometimes the task is just to carry out a review of the literature as a dissertation in its own right. So let's begin with definitions.

Terminology used in this book

We need to have a common language to describe the different styles of literature review. Throughout the book we have labelled our two styles of review as 'traditional literature review' and 'systematic review' to differentiate them, although in practice the boundaries can be less marked. We will examine these two styles of review and then consider the word 'systematic' because this notion is often misunderstood and hence misused.

Task

Look at the research method textbooks you are using and see how the term 'literature review' is defined.

Traditional literature review

A literature review is a written appraisal of what is already known – existing knowledge on a topic – with no prescribed methodology. Later in the book you will see that this basic model of a literature review can be complemented by a more scientifically prescribed model, the systematic review. Figure 1.1 represents the two types as ends of a continuum.

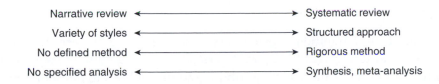

Narrative review ⟷ Systematic review
Variety of styles ⟷ Structured approach
No defined method ⟷ Rigorous method
No specified analysis ⟷ Synthesis, meta-analysis

Figure 1.1 A continuum of literature review approaches

How is the literature review defined in other textbooks? The two examples which follow are taken from business research textbooks. First, Jankowitz (2005) emphasises the process of building on existing work, but with a focus on *describing* and then bringing the work together in a *critical* way. This illustrates a use of the concept or term 'critical'.

> There is little point in reinventing the wheel. Whatever your epistemology, the work that you do is not done in a vacuum, but builds on the ideas of other people who have studied the field before you. This requires you to *describe* what has been published and to marshal the information in a relevant and *critical* way. (Jankowitz, 2005: 161, emphasis added)

Writing at the same time, Blumberg et al. (2005, emphasis added) discuss the literature review and here the emphasis is on individual contribution – as interpretation: 'An academic document which must have a logical structure, the aim and objectives and purpose need to be clear to the reader – it is an appropriate *summary* of previous work. But it needs an added dimension – your *interpretation*'.

Example 1.1 provides selected sentences from an article showing how the authors classify their review as a thematic analysis and state why it is not a systematic review.

Example 1.1

Recognising a traditional review. Extract taken from: 'Is the increasing policy use of Impact Assessment (IA) in Europe likely to undermine efforts to achieve healthy public policy?' (Smith et al., 2010)

This is an essay that provides a thematic analysis of literature concerning IA and associated tools and a related assessment of the European Union's new integrated IA tool (2010: 478).

This essay takes a public health perspective in interpreting literature that critically examines Impact Assessment (IA) and related tools (namely cost–benefit analysis, CBA), which share the same basic elements as IA. This body of work is vast, divergent and largely theoretical, and *not, therefore, appropriate for a traditional systematic review.* (2010: 480, emphasis added)

Systematic review

As a contrast to a traditional review, a systematic review has been defined by Petticrew and Roberts (2006: 2) as: 'A *method* of making sense of large bodies of information, and a means to contributing to the answers to questions about what works and what does not.'

We therefore define a systematic review as a review with a clear stated purpose, a question, a defined search approach, stating inclusion and exclusion criteria, producing a qualitative appraisal of articles. Example 1.2 illustrates a systematic review.

The systematic review method is prescribed. In this book (see Chapter 7), we describe six essential stages of methodology that you should work through in undertaking a systematic review:

1 Define the research question.
2 Design the plan.
3 Search for literature.
4 Apply exclusion and inclusion criteria.
5 Apply quality assessment.
6 Synthesis.

What does systematic mean?

Now let us consider the word 'systematic'. To work systematically simply means to work in an ordered or methodical way, rather than in a haphazard or random way. So, as a researcher, you have to take a systematic approach to your learning and to your writing. But taking an ordered approach to doing your literature review does not mean that the review can be called a 'systematic review'. It is possible to claim that you have taken a systematic approach to obtaining knowledge for your literature review, but without working through the six key stages of a systematic review protocol (see below) it cannot claim to be a systematic review.

Example 1.2

Recognising a systematic review. Extract taken from 'Networking literature about determinants of network effectiveness' (Turrini et al., 2010)

Abstract

In fact literature on this topic has been highly fragmented, comprising a plurality of definitions, multiple theories, multiple methods and multiple explanations. This paper aims to review and classify previous theoretical and evidence-based studies on network effectiveness and its determinants. (2010: 528)

We want to emphasise again that the terminology of literature review is confusing and ambiguous because as a subject or research method in its own right it is still in its infancy, in comparison, say, with the volume of books on qualitative research. We might say that the debate is still at an emergent stage. It is only relatively recently that academic journals in some fields began to publish literature reviews, because the view prevailed that literature was not based on research. So you can expect to see inconsistency in the language that authors use. Without getting into too much detail at this point (because the detail is in Chapter 7), we use recently published articles to illustrate the differences in terminology between Examples 1.1 and 1.2.

Example 1.1 is a review of the policy use of Impact Assessment in Europe. There is no clue in the title that this is a literature review. The clue is in the abstract, which tells the reader this is a thematic analysis. 'Traditional' in this context is used because the authors report that they did not conduct a comprehensive search of a specific topic or question, but used an iterative approach to search. A thematic approach was taken to analyse the texts. So the process defines the type of review.

Example 1.2 is a systematic review. The example includes all the review method terminology that you will encounter in such an article, based on the use of a protocol. Do not be put off at this point. Throughout the book we explain the terminology. If you want more clarification now, take a look at the glossary.

So, there is no clue in the title or abstract of Example 1.2 that this is a systematic review, however the authors do provide a methodology section. The authors designed a four step procedure (although we recommend six steps) to review the literature:

1 They defined key terms (inclusion) and the studies that were not to be included (exclusion).
2 They used key words to identify and collect all existing studies, search bibliographic databases and follow up citations.
3 They screened titles and abstracts.
4 They reduced their data, generated categories and produced final interpretation criteria.

From these two examples you should get the idea and be aware of the difference between the two styles of review.

Different styles of review

In order to study styles and types of literature review we have been collecting examples since 2000. An interesting outcome is that it is not always clear from the title or abstract that an article is a literature review until you skim read it, as in Example 1.1. Those articles that do classify themselves as literature reviews can use a confusing range of terminology, which in some cases is not explicitly defined by the authors in the text. The range of labels authors choose include: 'a synthesis review', 'a narrative review', 'a critical literature review', 'a critical review', 'a review of the literature', 'a review', 'a systematic review', 'a systematic review of evidence', 'a rapid review', 'an integrated review', 'a thematic review', 'a content analysis', and 'a bibliometric overview'.

Task

Take a look at any issue of the *International Journal of Management Reviews* and explore the wording of the titles. They are all reviews of one sort or another, but this is not necessarily flagged up in the title and it is not always clear until you read the abstract and the article itself what type of review it is. Example 1.3 illustrates the variety of possible review designs, the keywords emphasised in bold.

Example 1.3

Various types of review design, from the contents page of the *International Journal of Management Review* (vol. 10, issue 1, March 2008)

- The structure and evolution of the strategic management field: **a content analysis** of 26 years of strategic management research (Furrer et al., 2008).
- **Literature review** of theory and research on the psychological impact of temporary employment: towards a conceptual model (De Cuyper et al., 2008).
- **A review** of the theories of corporate social responsibility: its evolutionary path and the road ahead (Lee, 2008).

Two styles or approaches

In the following section we examine the two styles of review in more detail, with most emphasis on the traditional review.

Traditional literature review

Traditional reviews are usually critical, not purely descriptive, but there are other types of reviewing; the type (or purpose) is often indicated in the article title. The approaches most often used are listed here, and a published example of each one follows in Chapter 7.

- A *traditional review* usually adopts a *critical approach*, which might assess theories or hypotheses by critically examining the methods and results of single primary studies, with an emphasis on background and contextual material.
- A *conceptual review* aims to synthesise areas of conceptual knowledge that contribute to a better understanding of the issues.
- A *state-of-the-art review* brings readers up to date on the most recent research on the subject. This might be a seminal work, so it could be a useful beginning to your research project.
- An *expert review* is just that, written by an acknowledged expert. This may be heavily influenced by the writer's personal selection of material.
- A *scoping review* sets the scene for a future research agenda. This is comparable to what you have to do for your research project. The review documents what is already known, and then, using a critical analysis of the gaps in knowledge, it helps to refine the research questions, concepts and theories to point the way to future research. It is also used as the first step in refining the questions for a subsequent systematic review. It is our contention that you should undertake a scoping review before attempting a systematic review.

These types of traditional review are often based on a personal selection of materials because the writer believes the original authors have some important contribution to make to current knowledge. What you, as a writer of such a review, have to do is to weave those contributions together in a logical, systematic way, to develop an argument or tell a story. This approach offers the scope to be reflective, but it may produce a one-sided or even a biased argument (see Chapter 4). On the other hand, one value of traditional reviews is that they often provide insights that can be neglected or passed over in the steps towards exclusion and quality control that are required in the systematic review model. This traditional review is the style of literature review that most undergraduate and postgraduate students will be asked to do.

The systematic review

Systematic reviews are a useful tool for those seeking to promote research knowledge and put it into action. As with traditional reviews, they can help to identify gaps in knowledge as well as clarify where no further research is needed for the time being.

The appeal of this style of review lies in its claim to be a more neutral, technical process, which is rational and standardised, thereby demonstrating objectivity and a transparent process to the reader. These features sit easily in a scientific framework but less so in a more open qualitative, interpretative paradigm common in the social sciences.

So, you need to select the review approach which is most appropriate for your research.

A critical approach

One concept we have emphasised so far is that literature reviews should take a critical approach. We return to this in Chapter 4. The academic task of doing a literature review requires you to think, and to think for yourself, but to do both critically. In a popular column in the *Education* section of *The Guardian*, 'How to be a student No 61', Swain (2009: 12) offers a useful simplified explanation of what is required from defined critical thinking: 'Proper thinking is about forming an argument or a critical analysis that you can back up with evidence and reinforce with appropriate examples'. Some students find developing critical thinking challenging because their education so far has been based on hearing, reading, learning and repeating in examination. Professors and teachers, and the knowledge of professors and teachers, are respected but rarely challenged. At postgraduate level, it can come as a shock to be asked to modify that reverence for current wisdom and see that 'facts' do not exist in themselves and that experts are not always 'right'. This can be very demanding.

Criticism involves analysis of positive as well as negative features. It means recognising the strengths and the weaknesses of research that others have undertaken and being able to articulate why and how you think their ideas or theories might be improved. Critical thinking requires the development of a wide range of skills, but these are skills for life and hence it is worth investing time to learn them.

Knowledge and literature

Another core idea that we have used so far is that literature review is a secondary analysis technique; it is a secondary analysis of knowledge. But what do we mean by knowledge? What is knowledge? Modern technology enables us to access more information. At the same time, it has meant a wider involvement and sharing of knowledge between academics and non-academics, between readers and authors. Just think of how online encyclopaedias have changed the way knowledge is produced by experts and added to by non-experts. More and more organisations in both the public and private sector are now knowledge-based businesses. Figure 1.2 represents two types of knowledge: explicit knowledge and tacit knowledge.

Explicit knowledge is formal knowledge that has been articulated, codified and stored in an accessible format. It can be readily transmitted to others, through, for example, encyclopaedias. It is systematic and can be shared and communicated. Explicit knowledge is mostly based on empirical research findings and is in the public domain. It is the literature that you will review. Libraries are reservoirs of knowledge and information and now the internet brings that store of knowledge to your desk. So we will all need to know how to access knowledge using modern technology and be able to judge the validity and reliability of knowledge for ourselves. Your library information manager can be really useful in helping you to navigate through the constantly evolving way that academic knowledge is managed and accessed (Wade et al., 2006).

By comparison, tacit knowledge is informal knowledge that sits in your head. It is unwritten (so no one else can access it), and often unspoken. This is a type of knowledge that we all have; it is based on our past learning from experiences, insights, intuition, observation, and it includes our beliefs, values and emotions. This is valuable knowledge that postgraduates bring to their studies which can help them take a critical approach to what is being taught.

Researchers draw on these two dimensions of knowledge through reflection and eventually interpret the work of others using their tacit knowledge reserves.

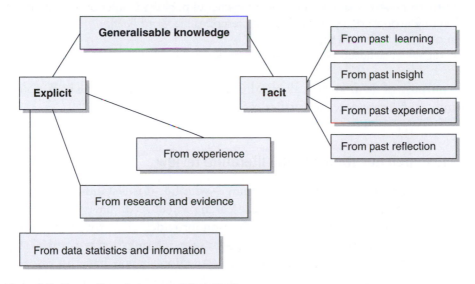

Figure 1.2 Types of knowledge — explicit and tacit

Why and when will you need to review the literature?

Literature reviews come in all shapes and formats, which we have tried to categorise as two main styles, with a subset of types, to make it simpler to understand. A literature review can have many different purposes and be written from a particular perspective. For instance, the review can be based on empirical primary research, on research methods, on theories or practical interventions, or it can be a conceptual review. It makes sense, before you start new research, to find out what other researchers have already done, because all academic work begins by looking at what is known already. A literature review might appear as the introduction to a report of new primary research or it might be an independent, stand-alone review of a topic. The following list gives a flavour of the types of situation when a review might be needed, recognising that each institution will have its own requirements.

There are six different scenarios when reviews are undertaken:

- In a research proposal (approximately 3,000 words), where the literature review would take approximately one-third of the total word count. This is a preliminary taster of the longer review you will write in your dissertation.
- In an undergraduate or postgraduate Masters research project you might have to review two different bodies of knowledge: (a) policy or theory, and (b) existing research.
- In a doctoral dissertation.
- In a journal article publishing research findings, which begins with 'stringing' of the literature review, meaning a stringing together of published material without providing any in-depth analysis (the journal prescribes the word limit).
- In a review in its own right.
- In an evidence-based policy development document.

The purpose of the review in all but the last scenario is to provide a background to and often a rationale for further research.

The research question and the literature review

Whatever form of research you are doing – whether it is a stand-alone review or the preliminary part of a complete research project – you have to begin with a research question. The research question provides the structure for the whole of the literature review. Defining your research question is a crucial step that points the way for your research investigation. If you have no research question, you do not know where you are going and there is a risk that your research will be unfocused. Therefore, automatically, a good research question will help to keep you focused.

- The research question will guide your literature search – it leads into the relevant literature.
- If the literature review is to inform a research project, then the question will be focal for the research design.
- The research question will inform what data you need to generate, how and from where, and finally, how you analyse the data.

For some students the research question may already be pre-set by your supervisor. It may be a problem related to work experience that you would like to pursue, but in most cases you will be expected to come up with some ideas for yourself. The best way to approach the question is to start with a general topic of interest. Explore, read widely, then select aspects of that topic that really interest you. Then focus down to formulate your research question. This will not be a simple one try and it is there. You will probably have several variations of your question. You may get ideas from reading what others have done already, since most research articles end with a sentence identifying gaps for future research.

There are standard features that your question should have:

- It must be clear: that is, it must be clear to you and your supervisor what you are asking.
- It must be doable: that means feasible, that you have the resources, the idea is not too big or vague in scope, and it is doable in the time that you have.
- It should connect with established theory and research.
- It should have the potential to make a contribution to knowledge.

Once you have formulated a draft research question, then do some preliminary searching. Find out how much literature there is and what it is saying. If your research question is too vague, it will not lead you into a coherent body of literature. Write the question down and then work through, as shown in Table 1.1.

If the research question were 'How can we improve household waste recycling?', the literature search has to look for examples of how we currently dispose of household waste and the problems that householders experience. On the basis of the findings, that is what is already known, you would design your research plan.

Table 1.1 Working through formulating a research question on recycling

What is the purpose of the review?

What style of review will it be?

Definition: How is recycling to be defined?

Research question: What are the barriers to recycling?

Questions to ask	Refine the question	Decision to make
Where, location?	Where?	Include all or narrow the scope
What sort of waste?	Food, paper, plastics, electrical goods, clothing textiles, furniture, other household goods	Just paper and plastics
Define how the recycling is to take place	Kerbside recycling, composting, black bin recycling, bins at community sites (civic amenity), charity bags, charity shops, giving things away for someone else to use	Just kerbside collection

So the final question could be: *What are the barriers to recycling household waste in the USA?*

Once you have a research question the process of review falls into place.

1   Formulate your draft research question.
2   Search for information, using key words.
3   Skim, scan, read, reflect and search some more, defining key concepts.
4   Obtain articles and read some more.
5   Reassess your question.
6   Formulate the final research question.

What is appropriate literature?

Unless your research topic is very new, it will be impossible to review every article, so you will need to select the most significant and relevant to your question. You might also need to access government or company reports, as appropriate to your topic. There are topics where you may need to be more adventurous in your choice of material, maybe looking at the work of different academic disciplines, because some of the best advances in knowledge come from bringing two or more separate fields of study together to create a new perspective. A hierarchy of sources of knowledge on environmental studies and recycling, for example, might look like that shown in Figure 1.3, which lists a range of relevant environmental knowledge sources from the top peer-reviewed journals down to the special interest trade magazines.

Peer review

Many teachers advise their students to access material only from peer-reviewed and highly rated top journals, but there are some circumstances when non-academic peer-reviewed information, known as grey literature, may be needed (Wade et al., 2006). The notion of peer review is based on a belief in the reliability of the peer review process, but you should be aware that there are some limitations and drawbacks to it.

If you are looking for insights and current topical issues, you can find them in specialist practitioner trade journals, newspapers and magazines – often half- or quarter-page snippets of information – because again these are current events happening. This type of material may not be included in your final literature review, but it adds to your working background knowledge and enables you to rapidly oversee the research field, set the scene, see who the movers and shakers are and give you ideas for new research projects. Eventually, with time, you will develop the experience and self-confidence in your own knowledge to be able to judge the quality of a source of information.

Source	Type of source	Rating
Business Strategy and Environment	Peer reviewed journal	Quality assured
Environment and Behaviour	Peer reviewed journal	Quality assured
Journal of Environmental Planning and Management;	Peer reviewed journal	Quality assured
Journal of Environmental Management	Peer reviewed journal	Quality assured
Resources, Conservation and Recycling	Peer reviewed journal	Quality assured
Chartered Institute Waste Management	Professional journal	Written articles, but not a rated journal
Journal of Waste and Resource Management Professionals	Trade journal	News and comment
Recycling Waste World Recyclingwasteworld.co.uk	Weekly trade magazine	News and comment
MRW MRW.co.uk	Trade magazine	News and comment
Letsrecycle.com	Blog	News and comment
Environwise	Weekly newsletter	News and comment
Local Authority Recycling Advisory Committee	Newsletter	News and comment

Figure 1.3 Potential sources of knowledge in environmental studies

When we submit work to an academic journal it is sent out to two or three appropriate reviewers, who assess the quality of the work and its contribution to knowledge. This is a helpful process because reviewers usually suggest ways in which the paper can be improved or where points need to be clarified.

The downside of peer review is that being judged by experts who have established perspectives and paradigms can act as a barrier to publishing new and unconventional ideas. What is known as 'group think' or consensus among academics can arise, which can be difficult to break down. The result is that there is less likely to be what is known as a paradigm shift, or a fresh movement away from accepted thinking towards a new direction. This is one form of what might be called publication bias, but another form of publication bias is when researchers themselves do not share their findings and ideas with the wider research community, they keep negative or uninteresting findings in their filing cabinet. The effect is to skew knowledge in favour of positive findings only, instead of having a balanced presentation. The peer review process of the past (150 years ago) tells us that Darwin's theory of evolution and natural selection would not have been published if subjected to review by his peers because it challenged the current paradigm, that is, the set of beliefs most people held at that time about the theory of evolution.

When we are teaching, we say that peer-reviewed journals are the best source to use because they are peer reviewed and therefore have gone through a vetting and improvement phase. Thus quality is assured. However, sometimes that process falls down, as in the case of the famous MMR paper in *The Lancet*, which was later withdrawn by the journal (Murch et al., 2004). It is notable that poor work is less frequently challenged in non-clinical research fields and it is less likely that papers will be withdrawn after publication. The standard of journal rankings is also a benchmark against which to assess work, although the benchmarking system and listing is open to challenge.

A note on peer review and journal ratings

As academics, we are encouraged to publish our research in highly rated journals. We then pass on this advice to postgraduate and doctoral students who need to publish their work. The first point here is to understand how journals become rated. Plos Medicine Editors (2006) [Public Library of Science, an open access journal] discuss the contentious nature of the impact factor game. For those who are interested, the impact factor is calculated by the equation shown in Figure 1.4. Later, Plos Medicine Editors (2007) write that 'even though the scientific skill of peer review is ill-defined, somehow peer review has become a badge of respectability among journals'.

Journal X's 2005 impact factor = $\dfrac{\text{Citations in 2005 (in journals indexed by Thompson Scientific) to all articles published by } \textit{Journal X} \text{ in 2003–4.}}{\text{Number of articles deemed to be 'citable' by Thompson Scientific that were published in } \textit{Journal X} \text{ in 2003–4.}}$

Note: 'Thompson are the sole arbiter of the impact factor game.' (Plos Medicine Editors, 2006: 2).

Figure 1.4   The formula for calculating an impact factor

Clearly, the impact factor depends on which journals and which article types Thompson Scientific deem as citable and the fewer the better (the lower the denominator, the higher the impact factor). A journal's impact factor can be boosted by the publication of review articles or the publication of a few highly cited research papers. But this measure does not tell you anything at all about the usefulness of any specific article in that journal, just that the balance is in favour of good articles in the opinion of reviewers and editors.

The second important point to make is that when undertaking a critical literature review we should be accessing all knowledge in all journals, regardless of impact status because our search is about knowledge. There might be an equally good paper in a lower rated journal which could not get past the strict publication criteria and the sheer volume of articles that are submitted. There is also a time factor. Sometimes a paper can take two or three years to be published in highly rated journals, so some authors deliberately seek to publish in lesser rated journals so that their work can be in the public domain. Readers have to judge the relevance and quality of the article for themselves. Only you can judge the relevance of an article to your literature review topic. In later chapters we introduce some of the standard tools which have been developed to assist in assessing quality.

Choosing which style of review: a traditional narrative review or a systematic review?

How do you know which type of review you should do? This depends on the assignment that you have been given.

The current zeitgeist in public policy and research favours systematic review over traditional review. It could be argued that the advance of online publishing has made it easier to track and obtain articles than when we had to identify them manually and send for a paper copy through interlibrary loans. The desk technology and computer software enhances the number crunching potential, thereby making it easier for reviewers to code and rank articles. This becomes almost a form of literature audit. In Chapter 7, Example 7.7 is a meta-narrative mapping systematic review which illustrates this point. It really depends on what you want from your review. Make sure that you do the right kind of review for your purpose.

The challenge to traditional review

The A–Z of Social Research (Miller and Brewer, 2003) contains a section on literature searching and systematic review, but not on traditional review.

Unfortunately, it is difficult to find any written support for the traditional review against the powerful surge of the proponents of systematic review. Advocates of systematic review are dismissive of traditional reviews (sometimes labelled traditional narratives), stating that they lack transparency of method and therefore cannot be replicated (Petticrew and Roberts, 2006). But as teachers, we know that at the beginning of their research many students have not yet developed sufficient working knowledge of their topic and are therefore not ready to undertake a systematic review. Hence our motivation in writing a textbook that tries to gives preference to neither one nor the other, but rather shows them as being of equal value but different or sequential processes. So our advice is, if you have time, begin by doing a traditional (scoping) review before attempting to produce a systematic review.

The main challenge to the traditional style is based on a critique of the process. Critics assert that the design and method for a traditional review is too open and flexible. One key difference is that in a traditional review there is no obligation to provide a method report; you only have to tell the reader the purpose of the review, you do not have to tell the reader how you identified sources, what you included and what you excluded and why.

Project management

Doing a literature review is time consuming. So be prepared to allocate sufficient time to do it. For any research study it is good practice to draw up a time plan. A Gantt chart is a time plan for a research project. This is a schedule of work which shows the various steps of an entire research project broken down into tasks. Figure 1.5 shows the Gantt chart of a three month long commissioned research project. The research and review phases are shaded. Planning and time management are important skills for researchers. The Gantt chart is a flexible tool because it helps you manage the process. You will find that your research will not match the time plan exactly, but it will help you to complete on time.

Finally, this introductory overview is a good place to suggest that you should set up a system for recording and storing your work. If you are working on paper, you need to establish a system for keeping your work in order. Some people prefer coloured card folders for different themes, topics or issues. In addition, the use of colour highlighter pens helps when you need to re-find sections or sentences or references in the material. Remember, you can adapt your method of data storage and analysis retrieval to suit your own learning style. If your work is stored electronically, set up a system of folders and files that enable you to work effectively.

No.	ACTIVITY/TASK	2009										
		Feb				March					April	
		2	9	16	23	2	9	16	23	30	6	13
1	**Commissioning and monitoring**											
a	Internal contract meetings		■									
b	Contract strategic development		■									
c	Scoping/negotiation with client		■									
d	Supervision and project management		▓	▓	▓	▓	▓	▓	▓	▓		
2	**Conceptualisation and design**											
a	Project Conceptualisation and design		■	■								
b	Focus group design		■	■								
3	**Fieldwork**											
a	Recruiting participants, venues					■	■					
b	Focus groups							■	■			
4	**Data processing**											
a	Focus group write ups							■	■			
5	**Reporting**											
a	Report writing/editing									■		
b	Client meetings/presentation									■		

Figure 1.5   The Gantt chart for a three month research project using focus groups

Summary

In this introductory chapter we have concentrated on 'knows what' rather than 'knows how'. The terminology to describe literature reviews is confusing and contradictory so we have tried to establish a common terminology as we explain the traditional literature review and the systematic review, using examples to illustrate the difference. We have labelled them as two styles of review. Within each style there are various types of review. We have told you that you should rely most on peer-reviewed academic journal articles, although there are also occasions when you may want to use information from a wider spectrum. There are flaws in the peer review system, limitations of which you should be aware. The remainder of the book is more about how to do a literature review.

2

SEARCHING FOR INFORMATION

Key Points

- Identify a range of information sources to discover where key information is available
- Develop online searches by identifying keywords and creating complex searches
- Search online and keep a record of your results
- Review your search

Be aware

- Sources of information are often written or compiled for a specific purpose and therefore may have limited content which may become outdated over time
- Seek advice from your academic supervisor and the Information Specialist in your library at different stages in your search, to cross-check the appropriateness of your approach
- Schedule time specifically for searching for information – it is worthwhile spending time at the outset to be sure you have a good range of materials

---

Introduction

This chapter introduces you to the main approaches to searching for information for your review. It emphasises working with your library and subject librarian. Not every academic library is the same, so invest some time in learning how yours operates. We have deliberately kept the guidance general, in the knowledge that working with online resources is a dynamic process. Most research methods textbooks will explain about 'the search', but the limitation of these books is that the information becomes out of date very quickly. Thus the emphasis in this chapter is on making the best use of your librarian to ensure that you use the most up-to-date and appropriate resources for your search. How much time and effort you can devote to your search depends on the reason for your review, as discussed in Chapter 1.

We begin at the beginning, with key words, and a reminder to record your search.

Developing online searches by identifying keywords and creating a search record

Identifying keywords

Subject librarians often refer to 'keywords' when searching databases. When you type in a search, rather than typing in a phrase or sentence, you will need to identify some keywords from your research topic. This enables the database to search for these words to retrieve relevant records. You might readily identify some keywords from your search topic – these are known as 'natural language' words. Natural language keywords are useful when searching the title, abstract and actual text of the article, allowing you to second-guess the words that you think will appear in these fields. However, at times, you will retrieve articles where your keywords appear in the article but the context is incorrect and therefore your search results will not be relevant.

In contrast, keywords used in databases are more deliberately selected and consist of a selection of 'controlled vocabulary' words assigned to articles by authors and database compilers. Controlled vocabulary keywords identify topics central to the article, rather than just words that appear within the article. So a good approach is first to 'guess' keywords from your understanding of the field and then review the keywords actually used in all relevant articles. This helps you to refine the keywords. It is therefore important to ensure that you become aware of the range of designated keywords for your topic in order to retrieve relevant articles. Your own natural language 'guessed' keywords may match the database keywords and help you retrieve articles. You can then refer to the additional designated keywords attached to the article to search for related articles. Many databases, such as ISI Web of Knowledge (see Figure 2.1) have a 'browse' facility so that you can browse words in the database. These are words in the database indexes linked to articles. Instead of typing in a keyword, you can browse the index and link to the related articles.

The following tips can help you to identify keywords:

- Select words from your research statement or research question.
- Identify similar and related words, for example, synonyms, broader terms or narrower terms (use a dictionary or a subject thesaurus to do this).
- Identify keywords and subject terms from the databases you are searching by browsing the online subject terms.

Constructing your search statement using your keywords

You can use the Boolean operators AND/OR/NOT to improve your search results.

Using AND

When you use AND you will be looking for articles containing two or more words within each article. For example, *employee AND motivation* would retrieve articles with both words in the article. You would use AND when you are searching for concepts and want to be more specific in your search (to narrow it down). You can also use AND to search for words within different fields, for example, a search for *employee* in the title field of the article AND *motivation* in the full-text of the article.

Using OR

When you use OR you will be looking for articles containing either one word or the other word. For example, *employee OR personnel OR staff*. You would use OR for similar concepts and alternative words or synonyms (to broaden out your search).

Using NOT

When you use NOT you will be looking for one term but not the other. So, for example, you might search for *broadband* NOT *wireless*. You would use NOT to exclude irrelevant results (to narrow down your search).

You can use the Boolean AND/OR/NOT operators together to search for specific concepts and synonyms at the same time. To do this effectively and undertake more advanced searches, check the help files of the database you are using. Each online database will have its own rules and helpful tips and tricks for improving your search strategy. Some databases will have a wildcard such as an * that you can use to truncate words. For example, *manag** would search for all alternative endings of the word, including *manager, management, managing*. Many databases also have a facility to search for words in proximity of each other, such as in the same sentence or within one or two words of each other. This can be helpful when the results you retrieve from a search using AND are too general.

Searching online and recording

It is always good practice to keep a record of your search activity and results. It can be a challenge to keep track of which information sources you have searched, how you have searched them and what results you have obtained. Keeping a record of searches enables you to follow up leads and it will save time in the long run. Otherwise you may find yourself repeating searches you have already undertaken. If you want to re-run searches at a future date, then you can also use the online search and save facilities within databases. As these facilities vary, it is important to refer to the online help files within databases

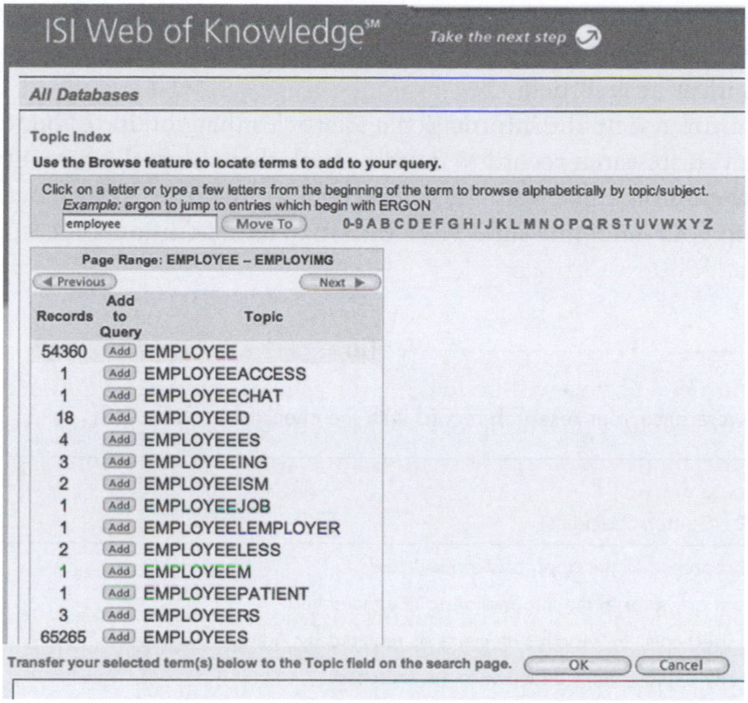

Figure 2.1 Browse facility on ISI Web of Knowledge

to see how to do this. Alternatively, you may want to replicate successful searches using alternative information resources. If you set up an online or paper-based folder for your literature review, then you can keep a research record, as shown in Table 2.1, to refer to, alongside saved articles or print-outs. This is good practice for all literature reviews, but if you are doing a systematic

Table 2.1   An example of a research record on 'employee and motivation'

Information source	Date searched	Searches used/scope of search	References	Comments/follow up
Business Source Premier (EBSCO Host)	12 July 2009	Employee AND Motivation AND review (limited to full text peer-reviewed academic articles)	4 key references	Need to try some alternative searches relating to employee satisfaction Also need to try on ABI/Inform Proquest
ABI/Inform	13 July 2009	Employee AND Satisfaction AND motivation	8 key references	Check for duplicates Follow up citations

review (see Chapter 7), the search strategy and the criteria for inclusion in your review is key to the quality of the data, and therefore each stage of the process must be recorded.

When you review the information and articles that you have found, you can refer to your research record to double-check that you really have undertaken a thorough search for your literature review. You can show your research record to your academic supervisor who may have additional ideas.

Tip

Cross-reference your research record with the checklist in Table 2.2.

Table 2.2 Search checklist

- Have I searched all the appropriate resources?
- Are there any gaps in the information sources searched?
- Have I used complex search statements as required by individual databases?
- Could any improvements be made to the searches?
- Have I identified all the relevant references?
- Have I used both full-text and bibliographic databases?

Some researchers use bibliographic referencing tools to collate their research. These are computer software tools such as Endnote™ or Reference Manager™, which are specifically designed for managing your references. Therefore, if you are undertaking research in the long term, you should find out what is available through your institution and obtain training so that you can use them effectively.

Review your search

You will know that your search is near completion once you have accessed many different information sources, tried several complex search statements, and the same key relevant articles keep appearing. Once you have the references that are relevant to the topic of your review, you will need to read them and decide which are appropriate for inclusion in your review. You will need to make reasoned decisions about which articles to exclude: perhaps on the basis of criteria relating to geography, time span, language, subject area covered and research methodology. For example, you may choose to limit your review to material published in the last ten years if the topic is recent.

How many references should I have?

Often students will ask how many references are required for their review, but I am afraid there is no right or wrong answer to this question. The point of a review is to provide a valid summary of the material on a given topic. Therefore, the number of references to include depends very much on the topic and the body of literature that exists on that topic. It is best to consult with your academic supervisor if in doubt.

In the process of writing your review, new articles may be published. You can keep up to date by setting up email alerts using the online databases, so that you receive emails when articles are published in particular journals, about particular topics or by specific authors. You will need to refer to the help pages of the individual databases to set the alerts up, as keeping up to date will be an important part of your ongoing research. You can also set up alerts to receive contents pages of journals. The contact details are listed later in this chapter. Now we will work through the many sources where you might obtain key information for your literature review.

The range of information sources available for complex searches

In the following sections we work through the range of resources available to you. This guidance will be particularly useful for postgraduates working on a doctoral thesis or undertaking a systematic review. As Wade et al. (2006: 92) noted, 'information retrieval is an essential component of the systematic review process, analogous to the data collection phase of a primary research study'.

Your approach to searching for information may combine any number of the following resources, as shown in Figure 2.2:

- Library catalogue.
- Digital library/electronic library.
- Individual full-text journal databases.
- Official websites.
- Online repositories.
- Bibliographic databases.

Getting started

All searches start with a topic. This may be given to you in the form of a research question by your supervisor, or you may have identified a potential

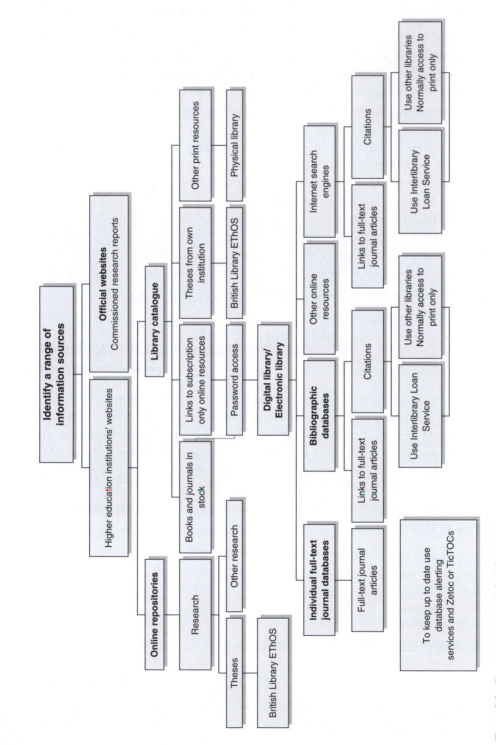

Figure 2.2 Resources to search for information

area of interest from general reading. You should realise that the exact topic of interest might become refined as you progress from general reading to a purposeful literature search, depending on the information you uncover.

Once the topic of your literature review has been established and you are ready to undertake a rigorous literature search, you will need to identify a range of resources to search for information. Remember that while a Google search in English on the internet will provide you with general information about your topic published by anyone, anywhere in the world, your library service will have search tools providing exclusive access to additional literature. These subscription-only tools enable sophisticated searching of all types of subject information. The range of library materials can be extensive, including academic, professional and trade journals, research reports, company information, government and official information, legal information, books, market research, financial and economic data, trade and press information, patents and standards, theses, directories and abstracts and bibliographies. If you restrict your search to the internet, you will miss out on content available in print in the library or online via your electronic library. Make the most of these tools while you have the chance, so that at a later date you can demonstrate your information research skills and knowledge in the workplace, where access to resources could be more limited due to much higher subscription costs for non-academic institutions.

This first stage in your research process is also your opportunity to reflect on whether you have previously used any resources provided by your library service, and if so whether or not you think these resources will be useful for your current literature review. If you have not previously used any resources, then ask your Information Specialist in the library for some guidance to get you started. Save yourself time by arranging an early consultation with your librarian – they will be able to provide you with advice to speed up your searches (as well as any passwords that are required), and help you to avoid the pitfalls of browsing the internet and the time-wasting that this can entail. As there may be valid reasons at a later date for searching the internet, they will also be able to advise you on *effective* internet search strategies (for example, using Google Scholar) to complement searches using recommended library resources.

Useful preparation for a thorough review is to start with a quick online search. Take one or two keywords from the title of your research topic and search on electronic resources you have used before. If you have access to a digital or electronic library search facility, then you can search one or several electronic journal databases in one go, by simply typing in a couple of keywords from the title of your research topic into the search boxes. Even if you only obtain details of one key article from this initial search, you can then use this to identify further articles by searching for:

- further papers written by that same author
- keywords the author has identified in their abstract
- articles in the reference list
- related articles listed in the publisher's database
- keywords attached to the article.

A review article which discusses previous published research about your topic can be particularly useful. These are things to look for in a key review article:

- Where do the important authors in the field work?
- What is the history of the topic?
- What is of current interest?
- Citations – who are the key authors in the field?
- Which journals publish this topic?

If you have not already identified a peer-reviewed article, your academic supervisor should be able to recommend one. Identifying a key article would be a very quick and easy start to your literature review. However, if you do not find any suitable articles from your first search, step back from the resources you have previously used and find out about the full range of online and print resources available to you (see the screen shot in Figure 2.3). Even if your topic is very specialised or narrow, it is good to identify and develop an understanding of the broader area of the research field involved. This will

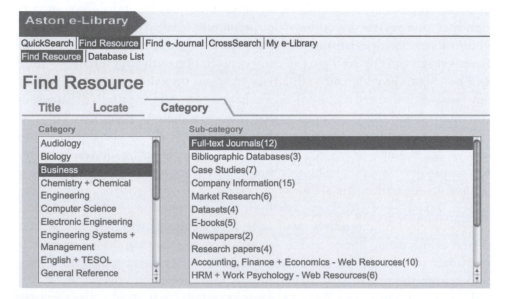

Figure 2.3 Range of information resources available

Software by Ex Libris UK Ltd. Used with permission. Screen image courtesy of Aston University.

help you place the results of your literature review in a wider context. You can then narrow down the search to your particular area of interest.

If you do not have a lead-in article or if you get too few results or too many irrelevant results, then you will need to develop your search strategy by selecting many resources and using several complex search statements. This will help you to understand more about the topic you are researching and is also good practice in searching online resources, where typing in one or two keywords will be required rather than using a phrase or sentence (see Figure 2.4 which shows a screen shot of key words 'employee motivation').

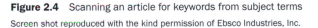

Figure 2.4   Scanning an article for keywords from subject terms

Screen shot reproduced with the kind permission of Ebsco Industries, Inc.

You should also be aware that correct spelling is of paramount importance so that there is a correct matching of your keyword with keywords in the database. You may need to rethink the keywords, or reconsider your topic. If you have a relatively 'new' topic, then there will not be a lot of material published yet in academic resources, so you may need to look at professional journals, as suggested in relation to environmental issues in Table 1.1. It is only once you have conducted a thorough search, and revised and revisited it several times, that you will know whether there is a considerable amount of research in the area of your review, or very little. It is a time-consuming process, but one that is essential as the basis for a thorough literature review.

Library catalogue

Many students approach a search for information by starting with the library catalogue. The library catalogue is an online index of all the materials held in your library. You will be able to use your library catalogue to search and locate print and electronic books available to you as well as reports or projects held in your library. You could identify a relevant key textbook in your research area and check the references lists provided within the book to identify experts and journal articles.

The library catalogue is not the best tool to identify journal articles for your literature review. If your supervisor has recommended a specific journal to refer to, then you can use the library catalogue to search for the title of the journal and then physically locate the print journal and index in the library. If the journal is available online, you may be provided with an online link from the library catalogue, so that you can search for articles online within that specific journal. If you access the journal, you can scan the contents pages yourself to look for likely titles and authors.

However, a library catalogue can have its limitations. Many library catalogues list the books, journals and other resources that are held within your library but may not allow you to search for or access their content. Some library catalogues not only contain lists of resources, but provide a link to your digital or electronic library and this would enable you to search for journal articles on a specific topic (see Figure 2.5).

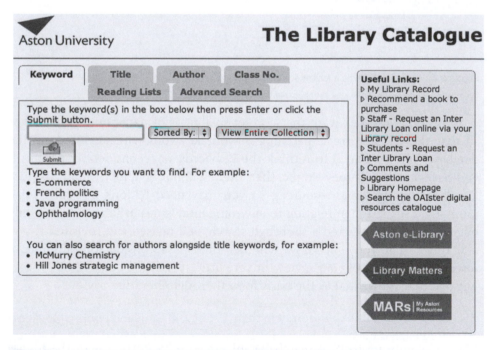

Figure 2.5 Aston University Library Catalogue and link to Aston e-Library

Software by Innovative Interfaces, Inc. Used with permission. Screen image courtesy of Aston University.

Digital library/electronic library

If you choose to search for journal articles from your library's digital or electronic library, then this will normally enable you to search across a number of different information resources, which have been pre-selected by your library staff. This can be really useful for initial undergraduate research for assignment topics, but because the databases have been pre-selected and the search tools are limited, only a few of the most relevant articles from each database will be retrieved.

Look at Figure 2.6. It shows the screen shot of a search for 'employee motivation' across several business journal databases. The central column shows the search as it takes place and the right-hand columns state the number of articles found and those retrieved. Beware: many may not be the most relevant. This approach, while being a quick starting point, will not be comprehensive enough for a literature review.

Aston e-Library

QuickSearch | Find Resource | Find e-Journal | CrossSearch | My e-Library
Search | Results

QuickSearch

Search for "employee motivation" in "Business + Economics"

Se		View retrieved		Cancel
Database Name	Status		Found	Retrieved
ABI/INFORM Global (ProQuest)	FETCHING		9627	
ABI/INFORM Trade & Industry (ProQuest)	DONE		2692	30
Business Source Premier (EBSCO)	SEARCHING			
Emerald Fulltext	DONE		9435	30
JSTOR Business	DONE		4734	30
ScienceDirect	SEARCHING			
SwetsWise	DONE		246	30
EconLit with Full Text (EBSCO)	SEARCHING			

Figure 2.6   Aston e-Library QuickSearch results

Software by Ex Libris UK Ltd. Used with permission. Screen image courtesy of Aston University.

There are complex search tools available within individual databases that help improve your search results. At postgraduate level, for a Masters or doctorate level review, it is therefore worth investing the time and energy to select and search each database individually. It is important to access individual databases via your electronic library rather than through a web search so that you are 'authenticated' as a library user.

To access your electronic library, you will be asked for a username and password, and this will ensure that you can access subscription-only services off-campus, where available. You can identify relevant databases through your electronic library via a list of databases in different subject areas. This will include information about scope and coverage for each resource. You can ensure that you are searching each resource in the most effective way by referring to the online search tips within the chosen database, for example see Figure 2.7. This will take longer than searching across several resources in one go, but the results will be superior because search tools that cover several online resources will not retrieve all published articles in your field of interest. They work on ranking systems that only retrieve the most relevant results based on a match of the keywords you have used.

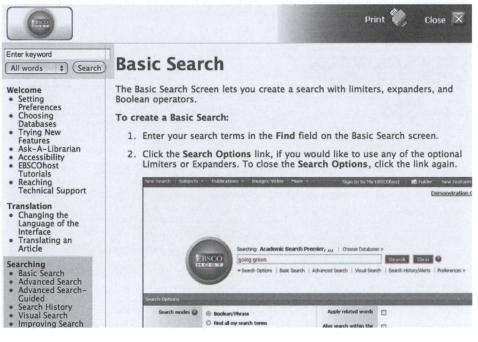

Figure 2.7 EBSCOhost online help pages

Screen shot reproduced with the kind permission of Ebsco Industries, Inc.

Individual full-text journal databases

Full-text journal databases provide you with quick and easy access to journal articles available in full text online, for specific publications. They are purchased by libraries to provide users with full access to the article. You will also often be able to follow the references of relevant articles, through to further full text articles, either on the same database or through another online service. You can search for keywords within the title of the article or within the abstract or the full text of the article. Once you find a relevant article, the full-text journal databases will also provide you with links to related articles, based on the keywords or references of the relevant article. Look for the cited references list attached to a relevant article. This will be in the brief search results or in the web page view of the article, rather than the portable document file version. This will often contain hypertext links to the referenced articles (see Figure 2.8).

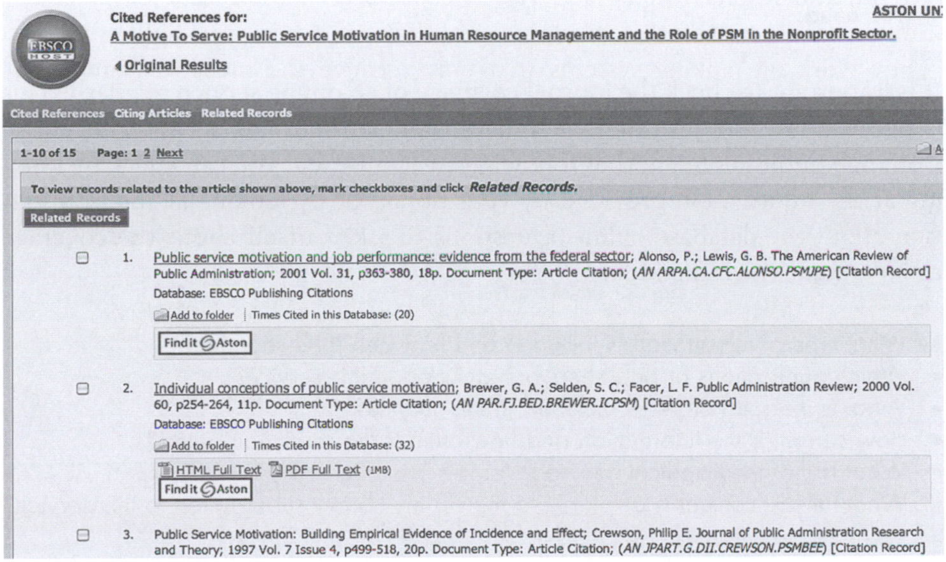

Figure 2.8 Using Cited References list from relevant article to locate further journal articles

Screen shot reproduced with the kind permission of Ebsco Industries, Inc.

Databases which give you access to full texts of published articles provide easy access to information, *but* you must realise that the databases are themselves limited in scope. They do not provide comprehensive and complete coverage of all information available in a given area. For example, Emerald provides you with electronic access to Emerald journals only, and Science Direct hosts Elsevier journals.

Thus, most full-text journal databases will provide the content of a predefined set of journals and these may or may not include articles about your topic. These services can contain an extensive range of journals or a smaller offering of journals, depending on the service, but do not expect any one service to contain all the articles of literature in your area of interest. In addition, your library may only purchase a subset of the material that is available through any one publisher. That is why it is important for you to be aware of the scope and limitations of all databases and for you to be prepared to search several in your subject.

There are some potential problems if you limit your search to full-text journal electronic databases:

- The databases may not contain the most recent issues of the journals you are interested in – your search would not be 'up to date'. If this is the case, check to see if your library has a subscription to the journal of interest as you will access recent editions in this way.
- The databases may not contain all the relevant journals for your field. You may have to search more than one database or locate libraries which subscribe to the journals you need.

It is important to check the journal coverage of an online service regularly. This is because the content can change over time and journals occasionally move from one publisher to another following an acquisition. You can check by looking at the information provided by your library or by looking at the information about the database online. Questions to ask yourself about the coverage of a database might include:

- What type of information is included and how can it be searched?
- Which publications or publishers are included in this service?
- What is the span of years included in this service?
- How current is the information and how often is the service updated?
- What is the geographical coverage?
- What full-text content is available to me via my library subscription to this service?

To summarise, full-text journal databases can be effectively searched individually, but they are not comprehensive. Different databases will complement the content of other databases.

Some online journal databases (for example, Sage or Taylor & Francis) will include abstracts and the full text of all published issues of specified journals, available *either* in print or online. Other online journal databases may include abstracts and the full text of the online editions available through that service only. In order to search for earlier articles from previous issues of journals, which may be available online through other services, or in print only, then additional services may be needed which go much further back in time. Examples of such services are:

- JSTOR ('Trusted Archives for Scholarship'), which only publishes archival issues and therefore will not allow you to search for the most up-to-date information.
- Bibliographic databases, such as ISI Web of Knowledge. This includes the frequently used Science Citation Index Expanded which provides citations of articles from the 1900s.

We have mentioned the problems with ensuring that your search identifies up-to-date references, but you may also find difficulties in accessing important articles from the past if you limit your search to online digital resources. Online publishing of journals commenced in the early 1990s and although earlier issues of articles are being digitised, there may be many excellent articles that predate the 1990s which are only available in print. If these articles are not available in your library, you will need to use the interlibrary loan service to request a print copy.

Official websites and online repositories

The biggest potential disadvantage of searching the internet for research information is the difficulty in critically evaluating the material found. This can be counteracted by using an academic search engine, such as Google Scholar (http://scholar.google.com) Scirus (www.scirus.com) or Scientific WebPlus (http://scientific.thomsonwebplus.com/), which can be used for scientific information. These search engines allow you to focus your internet search on the academic research available online although you will still need to evaluate the resources you find. As these search engines will also search content in subscription-only databases, make sure you log-in to your own electronic library services before you do an internet search so that you can follow links to full-text articles where they are available.

Articles within subscription full-text journal databases normally have the advantage of being verified through a quality-control peer review process. This helps to ensure the academic level and reliability of the research articles published within these databases. However, official websites and well-regarded open access websites can also be searched for additional papers or documents. Some examples include:

- Government websites (using advanced internet search options to limit to domain name .gov), for example: *defra.gov*
- Cordis: the gateway to European research and development (www.cordis.europa.eu/home_en.html)
- BioMed Central: the open access publisher (www.biomedcentral.com/)
- HighWire Press at Stanford University (www.highwire.stanford.edu/).

Many academic institutions also provide open access repositories to share academic research output (see Figure 2.9 for an example). This can be an additional source of information once you have identified experts in the field and their institutional affiliation. To access these papers, you would need to access the web pages of the institution and then search for the institutional repository. As the repositories are generally 'open access' they are freely available for

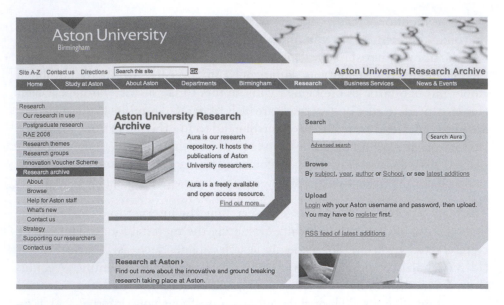

Figure 2.9   Aston University Research Archive: Aura

Software by EPrints Services, screen image courtesy of Aston University.

universal searching. Alternatively, you could search the Registry of Open Access Repositories: ROAR (http://roar.eprints.org/) to locate repositories worldwide.

Bibliographic databases – why they are essential

Bibliographic databases are a further key source of information. They provide a search interface for articles, keywords and references covering many publishers across a wide geography and a wide time span. Whereas full-text databases provide access to specific articles hosted by content aggregators or individual publishers, bibliographic databases cover the content of many publishers. Their main advantage is the wealth of data included in the databases and their citation-linking facilities, which enable researchers to link to referenced articles. The content of bibliographic databases can be specific to particular disciplines or multidisciplinary. For example, PsycINFO covers psychology across 49 countries, including journals, books and dissertations. PubMed covers biomedical and life sciences journals and includes more than 19 million citations. ISI Web of Knowledge includes several databases and is multidisciplinary.

The Journal Citation Reports within Web of Knowledge provides information about the most frequently cited journals and the highest impact journals in a field. The Journal Citation Reports includes science, technology and the social sciences and is a useful source for finding out which journals are the most important in your area of research.

Bibliographic databases should be used because they extend your search beyond your own library subscriptions to include all research published worldwide. They can also provide links through to the full-text articles if they are available to you through your library subscriptions. If your library has linking tools, through ISI Web of Science, you can link to the article you have located, to referenced articles and to articles which have cited your located article. This enables you to trace research backwards in time and forwards in time – an incredibly useful feature for ensuring you know about the most up-to-date research. This is also very useful when researching the background to a topic or following a particular theme and its development. This may seem quite a lot to absorb, so take a look at Table 2.3, which summarises the options discussed so far.

Table 2.3   A summary of the range of options discussed

Source	Pros	Cons
Library catalogue	Can search for print and electronic books. Can also search for recommended journals.	Cannot always search for journal articles about particular topics. Often limited to full-text library content.
Digital library/ electronic library	Very quick and easy to use. Can search across a number of different resources and link to full-text articles.	Search options are limited. Only brings back details of a limited number of articles. Full-text articles may not always be available.
Individual full-text databases	Self-contained resources with full-text articles always available.	Only provide a subset of published literature on a topic. Limited by content provided in each database. May not include earlier print issues of journals.
Official websites	Alternative source for official statistics, reports and commissioned research.	Need to identify which sites to use.
Repositories	May include papers not previously published.	Repositories are still being developed and as yet there is no central search facility for content.
Bibliographic databases	Can be discipline-specific and offer broad range of content coverage. Provide abstracts, links to citations and references for extending research.	Do not provide full-text (although may be able to link to full-text articles). Coverage is wider than library subscriptions so may have to order additional items via interlibrary loan or by visiting another library.

What do you need from a resource to make it appropriate for locating journal articles for your literature review?

Having described the range of options available, you should consider key features to look for. An information resource appropriate for locating journal articles should include the following features:

- Up-to-date (current, but archival access to earlier publications may also be important).
- Peer-reviewed (reputable).
- Comprehensive (covering a wide range of material in your subject area).
- Filtered (for academic-level research).
- Categorised (by type of information).
- Accessible from home (with password access to subscribed content).
- Quick and reliable search facility with linking options (for example, to cited articles, related articles, the full-text article).
- Easy to use (this might include option to save searches and set up alerts if new material is published by authors of interest or about a topic of interest).
- Ranking features (for example, the option to rank and sort results by relevance, date, subject).

Keeping up to date

As well as using the alert facilities within specific databases, there are services that are specifically aimed at keeping researchers up to date.

- **Zetoc** (http://zetoc.mimas.ac.uk/). Zetoc is freely available to UK higher education institutions, the NHS and other organisations and provides access to the British Library's Electronic Table of Contents of around 20,000 current journals and 16,000 conference proceedings. The database covers the period from 1993 to date. The advantage of Zetoc is that you can set up email alerts.
- **ticTOCs**: Journal Tables of Contents Service (www.tictocs.ac.uk/). ticTOCs is a completely free service for anyone and it provides the facility for you to set up online feeds for e-journals from over 350 publishers. Doctoral students will find the table of contents (TOC) service invaluable. Just sign up to the relevant journals and the update comes direct to your computer.

PhD theses

Unpublished research can often be found in PhD theses. You can search for theses published at your own institution on your university's library catalogue. Your university library may be able to provide you with access to the complete thesis in hard copy, or online if it is available electronically. To discover new theses written in your area of interest, then once you have identified experts, you can search their institutions' library catalogues or institutional repositories for possible PhD topics written under the experts' supervision.

To search UK theses across several higher education institutions in one go, you can use Index To Theses in Great Britain and Ireland (http://www.theses.com/) (a subscription-only service). This service provides information about UK theses going back to 1716 and up to the current date. Alternatively, you can use the British Library's Electronic Theses Online Service (EthOS) (http://ethos.bl.uk/) for full-text electronic access to more recent theses. For international theses, you can search Proquest Dissertations and Theses Databases (a subscription-only service) covering theses from 1861 onwards.

Once you have located information about a thesis you are interested in, you may be able to request access to a hard copy via interlibrary loan from the institution or an electronic copy via EThOS. However, it is worth noting that both Index to Theses and the Proquest service may not be completely comprehensive as they rely on individual institutions submitting information. In addition, the British Library's EThOS service (www.ethos.bl.uk/) only provides electronic access to theses from those institutions that participate in the service.

Materials not available in your own library

If your library does not have the specific resources you require, then you may be able to use interlibrary loan services or you may be able to visit other libraries to access the information that you need. Make sure you speak to someone in your own library to find out the next steps for obtaining information available elsewhere.

Summary

This chapter began with an introduction to the keyword phase of information search and advised you to keep a record of the search activity. This advice will be important to everyone who has to undertake a literature search. The literature search is so important for the quality of your review that we have explained in detail the many options that are available to you. For most of our readers, this information should complement the advice given by your own institution. Nevertheless, this chapter represents the first building block in your literature review process. Chapters 3 and 4 present the next building blocks, offering guidance on reading and making notes.

3

READING SKILLS

Key points

- You are reading for a purpose not pleasure
- Start by developing a process time plan
- Plan your reading time
- Think about key authors, time and dates

Avoid

- Superficial reading
- Too much in-depth reading
- Failing to record the bibliographic details
- Copying large chunks of text, instead of making relevant notes

---

Introduction

This chapter describes different aspects of reading skills which you might find useful. You are likely to read many varied types of non-fiction documents in order to write your literature review, and that is the same whether you are writing a traditional review or a systematic review. The material you are reading might consist of published literature reviews, or more abstract theoretical work. It could be purely research-based material, which in turn could be using qualitative or quantitative methodologies or even both. It might be project evaluation studies or officially produced policy reports. Whatever the type of document, the rationale is the same. You are reading for a purpose. You are reading for information and not for pleasure.

The concept of taking a *critical* approach was described in Chapter 1. Being a critical reader means making judgements about *how* an argument is presented in a text. You need to stand back from the work and have confidence in your own ability to be critical. This is usually achieved when you have a working knowledge and understanding of the issues and theories in a given topic. What happens is that you are able to move from surface (or information-seeking) reading to in-depth reading.

The key aspect to all types of material is that they were written with a particular purpose in mind and all tell a story. And that is what you have to do in your literature review – tell a story. So the skills you acquire as you read will automatically help you when you are writing.

Time

One of the first things you should think about is time – how much time do you have and how much of that time can you afford to devote to reading. Plan the time you set aside for reading. We all have different reading strategies; some people prefer to spend several hours reading, others find short, concentrated bursts more effective. When tackling journal articles you may find that reading is best done in short bursts. So that means you could read an article inbetween other activities. If you set aside at least one hour a day for two weeks you should be able to read at least seven journal articles. In Chapter 1 we introduced the use of a Gantt time plan for a complete research project. It is equally important to have a time plan which includes a section on reading. Use it as a guide to mark your progress.

Let us assume that the proposed time for the activities of search, scan, skim, read and write for a stand-alone review will take three months, or one term, as shown in the Gantt chart in Figure 3 1. The schedule of activities is set out, along with the reporting schedule and delivery dates, ensuring completion of the work by the end of December.

No.	ACTIVITY/TASK	October					November				December				
		3	10	17	24	31	7	14	21	28	5	12	19	26	
1	Decide topic	██													
2	Key words searching		██	██											
3	Scan and skim of text selection				██	██									
4	Reading and note making				██	██	██	██	██						
5	Synthesis								██	██	██	██			
6	Writing						██	██	██	██	██	██	██	██	

Figure 3.1 Gantt chart for a three-month project

Be analytical in your reading

The end point of your reading is to be able to write the literature review. The review will be based on your reading and your interpretation or analysis of the current knowledge. All the time you are evaluating what you read, reflecting on what is there in order to appraise the worth of the work, which means you have to read efficiently. As Blumberg et al. (2005: 177) note when discussing the importance of reading: 'Reading for review differs from reading for pleasure as it requires the reader to distil the relevant information and unravel the reasoning.'

Critical reading is based on critical thinking skills. There are several excellent books on critical reading (such as Cottrell, 2005) that are useful if you need extra guidance. Cottrell describes critical thinking as a process through which you have to move in order to identify another author's positions, arguments and conclusions.

Evaluating the evidence from an alternative point of view, weighing up opposing arguments and evidence fairly and being able to read between the lines is a skill that can be developed fairly quickly. In the following sections you will see two mnemonics (that is a system of rules to help your memory): first, the EEECA model, and then the SQ3R model.

First, the EEECA model, which gives five possible approaches to reading:

- **Examine** or analyse the topic – try to examine it from more than one perspective.
- **Evaluate** or critique the topic, thereby making a judgement about it.
- **Establish** relationships and show how they are related.
- **Compare** and contrast the ideas – are they similar to other work or how do they differ from other work?
- **Argue** for or against something to try to persuade the reader to agree.

You need to be purposeful in your reading and avoid getting swamped by anything that is not central to your purpose. But at the same time keep an open mind – always allow space for serendipity, whereby you may find something unexpected or unanticipated. So, be clear why you are reading, be clear about what sort of document you are reading and how you are going to fit all your reading into your project time plan.

Where to start

Be focused. It can be quite daunting when you are faced with a pile of text-books or a stack of printed-out journal articles that you identified during your literature search. So, take one resource, whether a book or journal article, at a time.

Process

The process is guided by two key questions:

1 Is this reading relevant to your study? Is the information appropriate to the matter under consideration?

   If yes,
   Continue.

2 Does this reading add anything to the arguments or information that you have already compiled?

   If yes,
   Continue.
   If no,
   Add the reference to your bibliographic list. Make a note that it has nothing new to contribute so far, add your reading date and reference details in case you want to return to it again. Then set it to one side in a colour-coded file. You will probably want to take another look at a later date for further examination, as your understanding and insight develops.

Tip

Remember this explorative reading phase is an iterative process (not a one off event): read, think and reflect, make notes, read, think and reflect, take notes, and so on.

Reading techniques – scan, skim and understand

It is known that surface readers take a passive approach to their reading, they try to memorise information so that they can recall what they read, but this approach lacks reflection and critical analysis. By comparison, a deep approach to reading means interacting with the material in order to understand it better. You have to be able to do both, eventually moving into deep reading.

- **Scan on the first reading**. Do a quick first reading to absorb the overall message. Does it confirm or refute, add to or contradict what you already know? Does the material seem plausible to you? In the process of doing this you are drawing on your own existing (tacit and explicit) knowledge, which will grow the more you read. With scanning you may search for a specific focus. Move your eyes quickly across the page to find particular words, phrases or names. This is what we do when reading a newspaper or magazine.

- **Skim on the second reading**. Read more carefully this time, taking in details. Note or highlight with colour pens, or underline any particularly relevant sentences or paragraphs or concepts that you will want to use. Skim reading is to get a better idea of what is there. Read quickly to get the main points but skip over the details. Check that the document is still relevant to your needs.
- **Understand in the third reading**. By now you should be able to react to what you have read, and agree or argue with the author's position or stance. Understanding the detail is when you read every word to extract information accurately.

This section suggests that you read not just to look for facts but to look for interpretation. You want to see what the text says as well as how the author has presented the material. What perspective is dominant? What is the author's paradigm? You will be familiar with the idea of research paradigms, such as positivist or interpretivist, from your research methodology course. A paradigm is a way of seeing based on a cluster of beliefs which not only influences how research is carried out, but also how research findings are interpreted. However, the paradigm may not always be discernible in everything you read, for example, conceptual papers.

So you might start with the scan – skim – understand sequence. Another way to approach reading is to adopt the SQ3R technique, a technique that is advocated in many textbooks (Ridley, 2008). This also refers to three different types of reading.

- **Survey** the text.
- **Question** actively and look for answers.
- **Read** – and read carefully.
- **Recall** – break the text into sections that show the main ideas.
- **Review** – look back to see if you have missed anything.

Example 3.1 is a reflective paper which considers current ideas in public health. It shows how to work your way through a text to see what it is about. The example shows you how to mark up key sections of text (my underline has been added to the text). Use Example 3.1 to practise your reading and marking-up/note-making skills. Use colour pens or underline or add square brackets [ ] to mark up sections of the text. As you work through the example, you could highlight each of the three stated aims in one colour, highlight the evidence in another colour, the method in a third colour, and so on. Cover up the right-hand column and test yourself. The right-hand column shows how the text could be broken down.

Example 3.1

Hanlon and Carlisle's 'thesis' speculating on a paradigm shift in human history, from a public health perspective (2008: 355-6)

Original text	Comments
Introduction **This paper has a number of aims: *firstly*, to consider the question of whether there are historical analogies with contemporary circumstances which might help us to make connections between past and present predicaments in the human condition; *secondly*, to highlight the underpinnings of these predicaments in the politico-economic and cultural systems found in 'modern' societies; and *thirdly*, to outline some of the questions prompted by this analysis, *and* to stimulate greater debate around the issue raised.**	The first sentence of the introductory paragraph (which is quite long and needs breaking down into its constituent clauses) tells the reader what the authors are trying to do. There are four separate parts (italicised here)
The arguments we present have been condensed from complex research and theorizing from multiple disciplines, in line with a disciplinary tradition of drawing on knowledge from other fields. We are, however, aware that there are some tensions between evidence and speculation throughout the paper and have, wherever possible, sought to ensure that speculation is plausible and consistent with the evidence.	Sentences two and three set up the authors' position and methodology. The methodology makes claims to an evidence base, and is based on a specific reading of existing knowledge.

In this way you can interact with the text, by taking a flexible approach to reading, rather than a sponge approach, which is soaking up everything you read indiscriminately. There are many styles of writing and some texts are not as clear as they could be, so you have to practice and learn by experience. Some authors use the opening sentences of a passage or section to establish their position and then follow up with the body of evidence and reasoning. Good writers will use keywords as signallers, whereas others do it differently and tell you the aim at the end of a lengthy introduction. However, be warned, there are some published articles where the reader has to work hard to find the aim of the paper and the position that the author is taking. This may not actually be a 'good' article, but if the paper is relevant, persevere.

Reading different types of material

This section offers guidance on reading books, journal articles and policy reports.

Tip

This last sentence acts as a signaller or trailer – it is telling you what is coming next. Look out for them when you practise your reading skills.

Books

These tips for reading a book can equally be applied to other sources of information. Never start by attempting to read every sentence in a textbook. Use the following list as a resource – like a toolkit.

- First read the title and publication date. Is this a classic, seminal text or a new one which might challenge the current state of knowledge or paradigm?
- Read about the author, usually to be found in the biographical blurb on the cover. Is this author an authoritative author or a new one?
- Study the table of contents, read the chapter headings and subsection headings.
- If it is an edited text (where different authors each contribute a chapter) check whether you need to read all the chapters or just selected authors. The overview or first chapter will summarise each contribution.
- Examine the book. Familiarise yourself with the layout. Look at the structure, the topic, style, general reasoning, data, tables and references.
- Read the Preface to see if it is by a guest writer or the author. The main ideas and contribution to knowledge are likely to be summarised here.
- The Introduction will give signposts for the layout of the contents within the book.
- Read the beginning and discussion endings of each relevant chapter.
- Interrogate – ask questions. What is your research question/s and how do they relate to this resource? Is this resource mainly theoretical? Is it conceptual or does it present the results of an empirical study? Many articles will contain some or all of these components.
- Check for your own keywords in the index.
- Check the Bibliography or Reference list. Do you already know some of the authors and texts cited? If you have just started out you will find several new references cited in the list. Later in the process, probably not so many will be new to you. Then you know you have a fairly good coverage of the key authors and articles.

Journal articles

The tips for reading a journal article are similar to those for reading a book. Journal articles are usually written by experts for other expert readers. Most published articles will have undergone the peer review process to assess whether they are suitable for the journal as well as to assess the quality of the work. If you are coming fresh to a topic, then reading a journal article may take more time than skimming a textbook. Lee and Lings (2008: 96), writing for graduates starting out on their research career, offer a telling insight into journal articles:

> Because of the word limits set by journals there is a need for authors to be clear and unambiguous (in writing for journals), which gives rise to a dense and very exact writing style, with much of the padding we take for granted in other types of writing (for example, in books) removed. This style can be very difficult to read because it is generally not entertaining, every sentence contains some relevant information that the author considers important. Indeed you may find that you end up reading an article three times, each time at a different level and with a developing understanding.

As with reading a book:

- Read the title.
- Carefully read the abstract and note or highlight the keywords which match your own, or possible alternatives.
- Identify the main argument from the abstract if you can (you may find this is not possible – not all abstracts are well written).
- Look at the structure of the work as this is the author's framework, through which the knowledge is communicated. Look at section subheadings, tables, diagrams, figures, pictures, numbered or bulleted lists, maps, graphs, charts. These visual presentations often summarise important material.
- If the article reports an empirical study, look for any hypotheses and read the research methods section.
- Look for the author's political, theoretical or methodological positions.
- Follow up the relevant references cited and listed at the end of each article.
- Examine the summary and conclusions in greater detail. Any gaps in knowledge, areas of new research needed and novel ideas might be located here. This may help you to frame your research question.
- Note again – you are not reading for entertainment, but for a purpose.
- Look for submission, correction and acceptance dates at the end of the paper – this indicates how old the actual research is.

Primary research articles

There is no set rule for the layout of articles in journals. However, medical and some research-based articles often follow a formula. In medical and scientific disciplines, this follows the IMRAD model:

- **Introduction** – why the author(s) decided to do the research.
- **Methods** – how they did it and how they analyse the results.
- **Results** – what they found.
- **Discussion** – what they think the research means and advances in knowledge.

Research studies based on primary research (new or field-based research as opposed to secondary or desk-based research) are known as empirical studies. They can be based on qualitative or quantitative research methodology, or they may be evaluation studies drawing on several paradigms and techniques. Table 3.1 summarises types of research design and the methods associated with each one. When reading a research article it is advisable to start by reading the methods section. In this way you are assessing or checking the validity, originality and importance of the paper – that is, its importance in the context of what we know already. If the methodology is vague, then you need to spend more time assessing the reliability of the data. In addition, note the date when the material was published and ask yourself:

- Is it the latest research or is this work now out of date?
- What was the research question and why was the study needed?
- What was the research design – was it appropriate to the question?
- What types of methods were used?

Table 3.1   Types of research design and methods

Primary research – the design usually consists of experiment, random controlled trial (RCT), cohort study, case control study, cross-sectional survey, longitudinal study, or case report. The methods are survey, interview, observation, group discussion. There are many scientific methods in experimental design that may be relevant.

Secondary research – takes existing data and reworks it, or asks fresh questions of it. This might be a simple overview at the beginning of an empirical article, a stand-alone traditional review, a systematic review, meta-analysis, economic analysis, or decision analysis.

Business tools – such as SWOT, PESTEL, Five Forces, Balanced Scorecard, EFQM, and marketing Ps are also used in management studies.

Grey literature: non-academic sources and policy reports

Grey literature is a term used for any document that is not an academic journal article. Technical reports, commissioned research reports, working papers, government policy reports all come under the grey literature umbrella (Wade et al., 2006). Grey literature is not formally published. It is typically written for a restricted audience and so is less easily available.

You may be writing a literature review which includes public policy reports. Many reports are written and published now by audit watchdogs, who are the scrutineers of public services, for example, the National Audit Office, service inspectorates and parliamentary select committees. The process through which such knowledge is collated is somewhat opaque and relatively little is known about how they work or what sort of evidence they produce to inform their conclusions. This section concentrates on how to tackle a UK government Green Paper (consultation document) or White Paper (policy report). Remember – this is a government-produced document and therefore it will have a political bias.

- Read the Foreword, which is often written by the Prime Minister or the Secretary of State.
- Read the Executive Summary before you begin on the substantial body of knowledge in the paper. This is the important substance that the author wants you to read. Official reports tend to have an Executive Summary, whereas academic papers have an Abstract.
- Look at the chapter headings – how is the material organised?
- Read the text, trying to read between the lines, to see if anything important has been hidden and excluded from the Executive Summary.
- Next examine the Bibliography, because that will point you to other similar policy work and illustrate which academic perspective, if any, is prominent.

When you read the chapter contents in a policy report you will be building on tacit knowledge, using your pre-existing knowledge to frame what you see. So ask yourself, does the new policy tune in with and confirm existing policy or is it announcing a major change of direction? If it follows a change of government, what strikes you most about the contents?

There will be new buzzwords. For example, in health policy, the concepts of 'upstream' and 'downstream' appeared in the White Paper *Saving Lives: Our Healthier Nation* (Department of Health, 1999) and subsequently became common currency.

Another feature of policy documents is that the tense is often in the future, noting ambitions rather than substance, as shown in Example 3.2 (see my underline). So, when you are writing and summarising the points you must remember to change the tense, unless you are quoting directly.

Example 3.2

A section from a government White Paper, the underline showing the use of the future tense (Department of Health, 2004)

The Government is committed to ensuring that measures to protect children's health are rigorously implemented and soundly based on evidence of impact. We <u>will therefore monitor</u> the success of these measures in relation to the balance of food and drink advertising and promotion to children, and children's food preferences to assess their impact. If, by early 2007 they have failed to produce change in the nature and balance of food promotion, <u>we will take action</u> through existing powers or new legislation to implement a clearly defined framework for regulating the promotion of food to children. (Department of Health, 2004: 36, Para 59)

Another type of grey literature is commissioned research reports. This is where research consultants (often academic researchers) are commissioned and paid by an organisation to undertake a specific piece of research for the organisation. The final research report will have undergone several reviews by the commissioner until an agreement is made on the final version. This type of document should be assessed carefully, because unlike academic journal articles or books, the work is rarely subjected to peer review. The final report may be the version with which the commissioners are happy because it meets their organisational needs.

Recording and note-making

At some point in your reading you will need to make notes. There are three main reasons for making notes:

1 To identify and understand the main points of what you read.
2 To help you recall what you have read.
3 To make connections across texts and authors so that you can rearrange them for writing the review.

More advice on note-making and writing follows in Chapter 4. Some of the issues that you might focus on when you are reading, and then interrogate the work by asking, are:

• What is the problem that is addressed by this document?
• What are the proposed theories or key ideas?
• How has the problem been investigated? What methods have been used?
• What are the results in terms of the problem stated?
• When was the work undertaken and published?
• Is it new or building on existing, older ideas?

This all helps you towards compiling your own review. Selecting what to write comes after reading each section in the document. As we suggest in the next chapter, you could set up your own standard procedure for recording information – known as a pro-forma (see Figure 4.1). If you write something down, it makes it easier to remember and to then go on to provide your own summary.

Finally, we end this chapter with a few tips based on our teaching experience:

- Style and accuracy – incorrect interpretation can happen as a result of over-focused reading or possibly an over focus on individual words.
- By comparison, lack of focus can lead to being too superficial. This happens when you are still skim reading when you should be reading at a deeper level, looking for keywords in sentences and not understanding the story or the context in which the words are embedded.
- This in turn results in failing to draw out the implications of what is stated – not understanding the big picture.
- Look out for dates. The extract in Example 3.2 was published in 2004; it makes a commitment for 2007. This current book you are reading was written in 2010. So you would be able to research and find out what had actually happened and whether these targets were met.
- Dates are important because knowledge is not static. When writers new to academic writing prepare a review citing 'out-of-date' information as current thinking, they have clearly not understood or carried out an up-to-date search of journals.
- Be critical. Don't believe everything you read – experts can sometimes be wrong.

Summary

This chapter should be of use to students returning to higher education after a break, who find the reading heavy-going and are not sure where to start. Doing a literature review is based on reading the work of others and making an individualised assessment or analysis of the work. This overview of reading skills emphasises the importance of allowing enough time to read and reflect, first, by noting the importance in terms of how you manage your reading time and, secondly, by advocating the use of a time plan. To help you read in a more structured and analytical way two mnemonics are recommended: the EECA and SQ3R models provide a structured approach to reading critically. Your approach to reading will vary depending on what type of document you are looking at. Although the procedures for tackling academic books and journals are similar, empirical research reports are likely to be presented in a more structured IMRAD format. Particular care is needed with reading and assessing grey literature and public policy reports. In Chapter 4 we expand on how you can move from your notes to writing.

4

FROM MAKING NOTES TO WRITING

Key Points

- Making notes is important, it shapes what you write
- Notes have to be clear, logical and written in a consistent format
- Learn how to spot bias in your own writing and in other writers
- The analysis should attempt to be original

Avoid

- Making no notes at all and trying to summarise straight from the original text
- Making notes in a random way, with no logical system
- Forgetting where your notes came from by referencing them properly

---

Introduction

You will hopefully have learned by now how to make notes from lectures – you listen and have to decide what is important, possibly with some hints from the lecturer and the PowerPoint slides. Doing research is different because you have to decide for yourself what is important. This chapter links in with the previous chapter on reading; it assumes that you have a clear research question and have started your search for information, using keywords to identify relevant papers or books. You have been reading, but it is at this point that many students find themselves overwhelmed by the sheer volume of material that they have printed off. That is why it is so important from the outset to plan your work within your time constraints.

Reading, note-making and then writing the review is an iterative process. Some advice on note-making was included at the end of Chapter 3. Here we consider other aspects that are important in leading you up to a finished product. Once ideas begin swirling about in your brain you need to capture them – otherwise, like butterflies they will fly away. So, get your ideas down on paper. Writing requires reflection and the process of reading – reflecting – writing will help you to clarify what you are thinking. Reflection is an important process in undertaking research.

Tip

Keep a notebook and pen close to hand at all times, you never know when the ideas will come to you, or something you have puzzled over for some time suddenly clicks in your mind.

When you make notes you are forming an opinion of each paper, an opinion which, at the doctoral level, will be original and hopefully innovative (in that as far as you are aware no other person has made the same interpretation that you have). There are five main reasons for making notes of what you read as you go along:

- To identify and understand the main points of what you read.
- To develop a way of rephrasing material in your own words.
- To help you reflect and think, concentrate on what is important and to recall easily what you have read.
- To make connections across texts and authors so that you can rearrange them for writing the review.
- To develop *your* own comprehension of the topic.

Note-making

Critical *writing* depends on critical reading, reflection and the interpretation that you make of the document. There are three levels of note-making:

1 Noting what the text *says* – but you can as easily photocopy or highlight a paper copy.
2 Noting what the text *does* – this is mostly descriptive, it covers aspects of the text and begins your process of reflection.
3 Noting what the text *means* in relation to your question – this is when you are really focused.

Tip

When copying text or quotations, always put 'inverted commas' around your hand-written or typed-up notes to remind you that they are copied and note exactly where that resource came from, especially the page number.

Recording text or quotations in the way outlined in the tip above should help you to avoid the problem of plagiarism. Plagiarism is covered in more detail in Chapter 9. One common error we all make when copying down a sentence or phrase from a text is to omit the page number. Nothing is more time-consuming or frustrating than trying to locate a page number to reference a quotation just at the point when you think you have finished. When you write up the review, the quotations will help to justify your argument, or illustrate the point you are making, but you must show where they came from.

Since your purpose is to learn, you have to make notes, and record the main points so that you can find the material again. Each person develops their own strategy for doing this. In essence, you are setting up a reading audit trail. This process can be done on computer, by typing up your notes and storing them as an electronic copy, but some people prefer to keep a hard paper copy as well as a back-up copy of the text annotated with the original marks.

Annotated hard copy

Some readers like to start to read without a pen in their hand. If you can avoid reading with a pen in your hand you will resist the temptation to copy huge chunks of irrelevant details down. Only make notes when you have thought it through. Typically, you can underline and highlight on your own paper copy in a variety of ways. You can:

- underline keywords.
- highlight different sentences or passages using coloured highlighter pens.
- use the margins to jot down questions you want to find an answer to.
- note keywords and concepts.

Whether you prefer making written notes on a separate piece of paper or on a computer, record the page and paragraph of the relevant passages so that they are easy to find on the second and subsequent reading and when you write up the review. Most people find it easier to remember things when they have written them down or have colour-coded them. When you make notes always number the note sheets and code them by topic so that it is clear where the information came from. Figure 4.1 is a suggested format for recording some basic information on paper or electronic format.

Electronic note-making

It is possible to set up notes pages in Endnote™ Bibliography, and then your reference details are together with the notes. Staff in the library or your institution can advise on how to do this.

Visual note-making

Another form of note-making is to use a visual pattern of important issues. This can be in a mind map, or it can be a table, or a themed or column-based presentation. Many researchers use mind maps now to manage their material. This is a diagrammatic form of note-making. They are sometimes called relevance trees or spider grams (see Buzan, 2003). The idea is that you start at the centre of the page and work your way around the paper, adding topics or issues as relevant. Some researchers like to put a flipchart on the wall and then stick on 'Post Its', which can be moved around as their knowledge and understanding evolves. This is a way of showing important authors, themes, concepts or theory. You will find your own preferred method evolves with practice, by reflecting on what has worked and not worked for you in the past.

Tip

Use colour-coded paper, pens and folders to organise your work in different subject areas. Another idea is to use separate pages for each topic. You can use closed boxes, circles, apple or heart shapes, use different colour pens, add in stars, or any other tool to help you visualise the information.

A colleague reminded me that if you have ever visited the office of an academic researcher you will notice that another tried-and-tested method is 'piles of paper on the floor or shelves' organised by subject and topic area. Each new note or document is then added to the top of the pile for later work. This behaviour is possibly a fail-safe way of storing information, an insurance policy against the frequent changes in technology and storage on portable discs, the most recent being the USB memory stick. But not all researchers behave in this way. Modern IT resources were meant to reduce the temptation to print a paper copy of everything interesting. It is highly likely that you will have a pile of print-outs when you undertake a literature search and review, so they need to be organised in some way.

The next stage is to begin to bring together and analyse what you have found out. By this stage, you should have highlighted paper copies and some handwritten notes, such as those shown in Example 4.1. But this doesn't bring your analysis together. Try writing one page for each text as this forces you to summarise into manageable amounts (you have to decide for yourself how much that is – 'manageable' is one of those weasel words that actually defies definition). You are trying to write a new and integrated interpretation, so try to be original by producing new ideas or conclusions. Summarise. Then, finally, put it into your own words. Invent a way of identifying your own words and observations, not those of the author, for example by drawing a circle in red around them.

Source: title of the article, author, date. NOTES: p1/p2/p3

Time:

_____

Place or setting:

_____

Method:

_____

Key findings

_____

Figure 4.1   A note making pro-forma

Table 4.1. shows the varying elements that could exist in a text that you might want to make notes about. The table shows where each element is likely to be within an article, so it is a guide to a quicker examination of a text. But there is also a warning – do not look just for specific information in isolation. You have to read the text critically to be able to comprehend the whole context and its conclusions. Note that Table 4.1 is a cumulative list in alphabetical order and not every document will necessarily contain all of these aspects. Be aware also that different disciplines will use different concepts (hence many of the terms in Table 4.1 are synonyms) so concentrate on the sections relevant to your own field.

From notes to writing

Context of time and place

Sometimes writers summarise the work of another author, so you will be reading it at third hand. Do not take everything you read on face value. Question the authenticity and accuracy. It is your responsibility to check whether the work has been accurately summarised and only the original source can provide that necessary quality check. Now, this type of checking may not be feasible for every original source. For instance, some material may be out of print or unavailable. Reading the original source is important if your review

Table 4.1 Elements in a text to look for to find the information you need

Column 1 *Introduction, problem statement*	Column 2 *Theoretical section or chapters*	Column 3 *Sections: chapters covering method, analysis, conclusion*
Definitions	Arguments	Conclusion
Events	Concepts	Design
Evidence	Evidence	Justification
Motives	Ethics	New research questions
Perspective	Hypothesis	Recommendations
Problems	Interpretations	Results
Questions	Justification	Summary
Standpoints	Styles of thinking	Techniques
Styles	Theory	

Source: Combined from Blumberg et al. (2005) and Hart (1998)

draws heavily on that specific work, and this does become more important at the doctoral level.

When reading and writing with a critical eye take care over the time line (ask when was the research done?) and geographical place (ask what was the setting and location of the study?). Think about the audience you are writing for – how relevant is the historical context or the geographical scope and the time line?

More about time

One aspect of time to take into consideration is the original date of publication of the work of a key author. Knowledge is incremental. What we know now has been built up over centuries in some academic fields, such as philosophy, chemistry or biology. In other areas of study, such as in the social and management fields, knowledge has accumulated in just a few years. When writing, it is customary to mention the study which was published first, to give credit to the author who made the initial argument, theory or finding. Some classical works were written a hundred years ago, but should still be acknowledged. This will vary with the academic discipline and the type of literature review that you are planning to write, but if you are writing about suicide, then a reference to the seminal work of Durkheim would be essential. You should, of course, try to take a look at the original works if they are available and make your own interpretation. Inappropriate or inaccurate citation of published research is common; it can perpetuate false ideas and mislead you and other readers. Your task is to critically appraise existing knowledge, but you may be misled if your appraisal is at second or third hand.

The extract in Example 4.1 illustrates how your notes can be used to write a more informative review. Example 4.1 is a paragraph from the literature review (limit 1,000 words) taken from a postgraduate research proposal on 'Dividend policy in relation to the use of executive stock options for directors' (the focus was the UK). In a short proposal there is limited space to expand on each document, so the point being made here is not to be critical of the original student writer but to show how a review can be improved with a small addition of words to become more informative. The paragraph is headed 'Dividend policy and its determinants'. This example is to look specifically at issues of time line and place.

Example 4.1

An illustration of the importance of time and place

This extract is a basic review paragraph on dividend policy and its determinants, taken from a student's original text, as submitted for assessment.

Dividend policy and its determinants

A few major theories have emerged in the attempt to unravel the dividend policy mystery. The clientele theory, put forward by Miller and Modigliani in 1961, suggests that investors chose to invest in companies with a payout policy that suits their tax situation and consumption requirements. In contrast, the dividend signalling theory states that managers' payout decisions signal to the market their view for the future of the company (Grullon et al. 2002 [student's original version has an error]; Michaely et al. 1995). Another possible explanation is offered by the free cash flow hypothesis. It argues that investors welcome increases in dividends because it reduces the control of managers by returning some of the free cash to investors. Thus limiting the amount of cash managers could invest in projects with negative present value (Jensen 1986). However, in practice, after conducting a survey on close to 400 companies in the US, Brav et al. (2006) [student's original version has an error] found that the views of management don't hold strong support for the theories presented above. (162 words)

My immediate observations of the text in Example 4.1 are:

- According to the anonymous student, we have five authors with three theories, with accounts beginning in 1961 and the latest in 2002. Using 'time and place' devices we can improve the work.
- The most recent paper cited (Brav et al., 2005) is based on a US study. On examination of the original articles (and from the journal titles) it is clear that all the papers are printed in American journals and all the authors are American. So one key point to make is that these are theories developed in the USA, but the student

study is about the UK. So one research question that can be asked – do these theories hold across economies?

- The studies cover research carried out over 20 years. So a research question could be: To what extent are the theories developed since 1986 still relevant in a 2009 economic context?

Authors

Roni Michaely's name appears on three of the five papers cited in Example 4.1 (Michaely et al., 1995; Grullon and Michaely, 2002; Brav et al., 2005). This suggests that he is a leading academic on this topic. So it might be worthwhile doing a name search to find out what else he has written.

Taking these devices of 'time, place, author' into account, the paragraph in Example 4.1 could be rewritten as shown in Example 4.2. My additions or changes are in italics and I have removed the original underline from the references.

Example 4.2

The Revised version of the basic review paragraph on dividend policy and its determinants from Example 4.1

A few major theories have emerged *from the USA* in the attempt to unravel the dividend policy mystery. The clientele theory, put forward *in a theoretical paper on dividend policy* by Miller and Modigliani in 1961, suggests that investors chose to invest in companies with a payout policy that suits their tax situation and consumption requirements. In contrast, the dividend signalling theory states that managers' payout decisions signal to the market their view for the future of the company *(Michaely et al., 1995; Grullon and Michaely, 2002). Michaely et al.'s (1995) work is based on an empirical study of dividend initiations and emissions for the years 1964 to 1988, using the New York stock exchange and other secondary data sources.*

Another possible explanation is offered by the free cash flow hypothesis. *This theory* argues that investors welcome increases in dividends because it reduces the control of managers by returning some of the free cash to investors. Thus limiting the amount of cash managers could invest in projects with negative present value (Jensen, 1986). *Jensen argued, taking the international oil energy market as a case study, that free cash flow theory of capital structure can also help to explain financial restructuring.* However, in practice, after conducting a survey *of 384 financial executives and interviews with an additional 23 to determine the factors that drive dividend and share repurchase decisions* in the USA, Brav et al. (2005: 484) *concluded that 'management views provide little support for agency, signalling and the clientele hypothesis of payout policy'.* (251 words)

Writing: critical writing and types of argument

There are many excellent texts on study skills which take you through the process of making an argument, some of which you will have consulted earlier in your academic career, for example in study skills sessions and for essay writing (see, for example, Bonnett, 2001; Levin 2004; Currie, 2005). The following section offers some key reminders of the common core concepts.

An 'argument', in this context, means putting forward reasons to influence the reader, supported by evidence. An argument (in the academic meaning of that word) is a form of intellectual engagement with a reader (or listener). It should be constructive. The point here is to persuade the reader with *your* argument. It is not an argument about the person (or writer), but it is an argument about the substance of the work, the ideas and assertions, or theory and evidence, or conclusions that an author has made.

Your review may contain a mixture of all these forms of writing – the ideas, assertions, theory and evidence or conclusions. Quite often literature reviews written by those new to academic discussion are marked down. This is because there is too much description and not enough argument and explanation, reflection or analysis. You have to put an interpretation on the work. Here we have listed six forms of writing which may appear in your review, although not all are arguments:

1 **A description or an assertion**: A description tells us how things are. It is not an argument. It is an account, always written from a certain point of view, to some purpose. A description doesn't explain.
2 **A model**: A model is usually a visual representation of something – it can be a flow chart or simple Venn diagram. Models are abstractions of often complex material.
3 **A theory**: A theory is a simple statement, usually based on a set of hypotheses related to a logical argument. If I do x, then y or z is likely to happen.
4 **An explanation**: An explanation tries to make something comprehensible and uses examples to justify why the writer thinks this way.
5 **An analysis**: An analysis is a critical account of the component parts or factors involved in something.
6 **Synthesis**: Synthesis is where you bring everything together, hopefully in a new and original way.

Making a value judgement and bias

Bias is a pre-existing attitude, an academic mindset of preconceptions and taken-for-granted ideas or knowledge that is often subconscious. Bias means having an inclination or preference that influences your judgement, so that your analysis is not balanced or even-handed. Another way to describe this tendency is prejudice, a concept often used in a pejorative way. To have a bias is to have a prior or specific disposition or attitude about something. The assumption that we can produce unbiased, objective and value-free research is at the heart of the scientific debate. We like to think we are impartial and objective – that is the positivist paradigm of science. But in reality it is difficult to shake off a lifetime of preconceived notions, attitudes and experiences – that is the realist paradigm. Subjectivity is the lens through which you look at the world. So, for example, it may be a feminist lens you see through, or a Marxist lens.

Tip

Write down now what you think your bias and prejudices are. Consider: can you set them aside when preparing your review *or* is it appropriate to your field of research that you recognise and acknowledge them.

Critique

Remember that to critique academically means to give both positive and negative points about a paper, and to recognise both the strengths and the weaknesses. Do not believe that just because something is published in a journal there is nothing to critique: no research is perfect. Most authors begin by focusing on the positive aspects and then, depending on the text, might note contradictions with other writers, or comment on the discussion, or note gaps in knowledge still to be tackled. See also Chapter 1 where we noted that the peer review process can act as a gatekeeper to new ideas being published. So you need to give a balanced review – one where the outcome is equally valuable. An unbalanced project is one where only evidence which agrees with your pre-existing mindset or expectations is presented.

In real life, criticism generally means looking for faults and passing critical comments; so it is a negative act. On the other hand, critical analysis, in the academic context of writing, is a positive process involving reflection and evaluation in order to determine the value or quality of something. However, you need to develop the skills and the language to draw the reader's attention to it. Examine some articles and see how others in your discipline have done it.

Table 4.2 is a critique by Gourlay (2006) which asserts that 'Nonaka's proposition is that knowledge is created through the interaction of tacit and explicit knowledge involving four modes of knowledge conversion' (2006: 1415).

Table 4.2 An example showing how a critique is put together: 'Conceptualizing knowledge creation: a critique of Nonaka's theory' (Gourlay, 2006)

The original text	Deconstructing notes on the text
In the Abstract	
The theory that knowledge is created through the interaction of tacit and explicit knowledge involving four modes of knowledge conversion is flawed.	This is the main point of Gourlay's critique.
The theory appears to have attracted little systematic criticism, at least not in management and organisational literature (2006: 1416)	This claim is based on an assessment of citations between 1994 and 2004.
The most far-reaching critique is in a neglected paper by Essers and Schreinemakers (1997).	Gourlay has found another critical article.
Another comprehensive but neglected critique (Jorna, 1998)	And another.
Jorna's critique centred on the neglect of previous research, while Essers and Schreinemakers', and Bereiter's critiques (Bereiter, 2002) were largely concerned with the consequences of the model.	This tells us why the others were critical of the original theory.

Some comments on process

Be prepared for lots of redrafting and rewriting. The literature review should be clearly written and well structured with subheadings. Introduce signalling words, or pointers and linkages (as suggested below), that provide a map to lead the reader through the evidence so that the ultimate conclusion is justified. Identify the main points of your argument for the reader. Experiment with the structure and sequence of your review to find the best way to illustrate and communicate your ideas to the reader.

The following are examples of signalling words (Cottrell, 2005):

- **Similar opinions**: similarly, equally, likewise, in the same way.
- **Strengthening words** (words that strengthen your argument): in addition, besides, too, moreover, furthermore, it is different, besides, not only … but also.
- **Alternative words** (words that argue against something): others argue that … (but always give a reference source for 'others'), alternatively, it might/could be argued that …
- **Rebuttal words**: however, on the other hand, nonetheless, notwithstanding.
- **Contrast or contradict words**: although, conversely, by contrast, on the one hand … on the other hand.
- **Results and consequences**: as a result, as a consequence, hence, thus, consequently, because of this.
- **Concluding words**: therefore, in conclusion, thus, we can see that …

Remember that the write-up may take you as long as the search for literature, the reading and note-making. Try to read your work out loud as this helps you to spot over-long sentences and/or incomplete sentences.

Summary

This chapter has reinforced the assertion made earlier that good critical writing depends on close critical reading, reflection and the interpretation that you make for yourself. When it comes to note-making, choose the approaches that you find most useful and convenient for your purposes. That may be using a standard pro-forma, highlighted or annotated paper originals or notes stored electronically. Your notes can, if relevant, include features of each document, such as the context, the time of writing and publication, and anything relevant about the author, such as the place of writing and publication. An example of dividend policy theory illustrates this point. Moving from your notes to writing requires you to make an argument and not merely be descriptive. Using signalling words in your review reinforces the way you lead the reader through your review and helps you to avoid producing a 'shopping list'. We will pick up on the writing up process again in Chapter 6.

PART 2

USING INFORMATION

5

THE TRADITIONAL REVIEW

Key points

- Traditional reviews allow you to be flexible and to explore ideas
- They can be insightful and original
- They can be undertaken by one person at undergraduate or postgraduate level
- Subjectivity is implicit; there is no protocol but it is good practice to tell the reader on what basis the material was selected
- It is only relatively recently that the literature review has been deemed a research methodology in its own right

Be aware

- The result depends on the skills of the writer
- Traditional reviews can be dismissed as an 'opinion piece'
- Traditional review is less helpful for policy development because it is not a systematic review (see Chapter 7)

Overview of the debate

So far in Part I of this book we have covered the early stages of doing a literature review. We have:

- identified a topic, funnelled down and decided on a specific research area and research question
- identified keywords and used the library resources to search for resources and information
- read the material, and
- made notes after reading.

Part II of the book concentrates on two different approaches to literature review. The language – or labels – used to describe literature reviews tends to be confused. So each time you read the words 'literature review' you should check, read and categorise what type of review it is. In this book we set out to differentiate between a 'traditional literature review' and a 'systematic literature review', which has a very specific meaning. The first part of this chapter examines a selection of published reviews showing how each one has a different focus. The latter part of the chapter begins working through the review process. To make the most of this chapter you need to refer to the original article because sometimes we quote from the original work and other times we only provide a commentary.

A literature review is a desk-based research method by which the researcher critically describes and appraises what is already known about a topic using secondary sources. In some instances, a literature review is described as a traditional narrative review (Torgerson, 2003) because it consists of a narrative style of presentation.

- The traditional review, as undertaken by undergraduate and Masters-level students, aims to be comprehensive, which means it aims to present a summary review of the current state of knowledge about a particular subject.
- The traditional review also seeks to add new insights on the topic.

Critique of traditional review

Some writers who promote a systematic review methodology take a pejorative approach to the traditional review on the grounds that it does not produce reliable evidence (see Petticrew and Roberts, 2006, on health and social care). Which approach to review you take depends on the context of review, the academic discipline of study, and the purpose. It also depends on what level of study you are at. Traditional review is the norm at undergraduate level. At postgraduate level traditional review may be less helpful for guiding policy or, as Torgerson (2003) asserts, for contributing to an informed debate of the issues in education. Critics dismiss the traditional review as of little value because it is 'non-scientific', or it is merely a discussion paper, or an opinion piece. This is because in traditional reviews the author's subjectivity is implicit; there is no protocol and quite often no description of how the review was carried out. In some journal articles, for example, there might not be a methods section to help the reader understand the choices made on selection or on the review process. The critique claims that the absence of a systematic protocol means that an uninformed reader is unable to judge the completeness of the arguments put forward in such a review (the systematic protocol is described in Chapter 7).

But the argument presented in this book is that before being able to move on to doing a systematic review you have to be confident in your searching skills and basic reviewing ability. To start with a traditional review helps you to develop those reviewing skills and gives you the insights to enable you to work your way up to doing the systematic review. It can be argued that this form of review is a 'scoping review', that is, a review which sets the scene for a future research agenda. It is unlikely that at undergraduate level you will have the time to do more than a traditional review, but that does not mean you do not need to know what a systematic review methodology involves. Postgraduates are most likely to attempt a systematic review.

Critics of traditional narrative review argue:

- that there is no formal methodology, so there is a lack of transparency and no academic rigour
- that the reasons for including some material and excluding others is not discussed
- on selection grounds, because the review is only a small, potentially biased selection of the whole range of literature on the subject
- since there is no methodological audit trail, the review cannot be replicated by others
- that there is no quality assessment of the material included; incorrect interpretations may therefore result
- that contrary or conflicting views may not be identified or included in the review.

When will you need to review the literature?

In Chapter 1 we suggested that there are six different scenarios when literature reviews are undertaken:

1 When writing a research proposal, usually for postgraduate dissertations of approximately 3,000 words in length. The review would take up approximately one-third of this word count. So this review would be a preliminary taster of the more in-depth review that you write in your dissertation. On the other hand, a proposal seeking funding for further research would be a review which summarises key findings before highlighting the knowledge gap, thereby justifying the rationale for further research.
2 For an undergraduate or postgraduate Masters research project, where the dissertation is between 10,000 and 20,000 words in length. The review might be one or two chapters covering policy or theory and empirical applied studies. This would be a more comprehensive review of the topic, still identifying the research gap and explaining or justifying the project.
3 For a doctoral dissertation.
4 For a journal article publishing research findings, which often begins with a summary or a section that 'strings together' the literature without providing an in-depth analysis.
5 When writing a literature review in its own right to provide a stand-alone review of a topic.
6 For evidence-based policy development.

Types of review: critical, conceptual, state of the art, expert and scoping

To recap, traditional reviews are exploring issues, developing ideas, identifying research gaps, whereas systematic reviews are compiling evidence to answer a specific research or policy problem or question, using a protocol. It can be argued that both approaches are used to answer a research question or problem. However, the main difference is in the design and the methodological approach. Within the traditional review model, there are different types or reasons for reviewing. The type or reason is often indicated in the article title. The types are listed next and then followed by an example of each type.

- A *traditional review* usually adopts a *critical approach* which might assess theories or hypotheses by critically examining the methods and results of single primary studies, with an emphasis on background and contextual material. The material is selected in order to present an argument. Example 5.1 is a paper on marketing recycling and is representative of a typical academic paper – setting up the story so far.
- A *conceptual review* aims to synthesise areas of conceptual knowledge that contribute to a better understanding of the issues. Example 5.2 is a discussion about the two concepts: public health and population health.
- A *state-of-the-art review* brings readers up to date on the most recent research on the subject. This might be a seminal work, so it could be a useful beginning to your research project. Example 5.3 is a state-of-the-art review of green supply-chain management.
- Similarly, an *expert review* is just that, written by an acknowledged expert. This may be heavily influenced by the writer's own ideology and paradigm. Example 5.4 is an expert review on organisational and managerial change.
- A *scoping review* sets the scene for a future research agenda. This is comparable to what you have to do for your student project. The review documents what is already known, and then, using a critical analysis of the gaps in knowledge, it helps to refine the questions, concepts and theories to point the way to future research. It is also used as the first step in refining the questions for a subsequent systematic review. The output is a document which maps out the general topic area and makes recommendations for future research. Example 5.5 explores the research agenda for research on firm acquisition.

To summarise, these types of traditional review are often based on a personal selection of materials because the author has some important contribution to make to the knowledge base and the point is to help develop an argument or tell a story. This approach offers greater scope to be reflective, but may provide a one-sided or even biased argument, as discussed in Chapter 4.

TASK

Take a look at the contents pages of recent editions of the journal *The International Journal of Management Reviews,* which publishes only review articles (note: some articles contain no methodology section at all). You will see that the article titles carry a pointer, indicating what types of a review they are. Sometimes they declare the method, as in: 'content analysis', 'towards a conceptual model', 'a review of theories', 'towards a research agenda', 'a narrative review'.

The key point about traditional reviews is that it is not necessary to conduct a comprehensive systematic search, but you will help the reader more if the method and selection rationale is described because they will be able to judge the completeness of your argument. So, we are talking here about a search description (building on Chapter 2), then a selection rationale, prior to analysis and synthesis. The reader can then understand better the relevance and importance of the review and its findings with respect to their own information needs.

Some examples of published traditional reviews

To benefit from the following examples you will need to read the original papers.

Critical reviews

Example 5.1 is taken from Smallbone (2005), an article entitled 'How can domestic households become part of the solution to England's recycling problems?' In this article, Smallbone is reading the recycling literature from a marketing perspective. So the critical reading skill here is to apply one academic perspective, 'marketing', on to another academic perspective, in this case 'environmental studies'. Example 5.1 shows you how this review is assembled. You can see how many articles were used in the review and that having an alternative focus helps you to identify a gap.

TASK

It would help if you can look at Smallbone's article for yourself to see how the review is constructed (you can find it online at WileyInterscience, *Business Strategy and the Environment,* 4(2): 110–122.

The first paragraph of the review (Example 5.1, column 1) is laid out to show how it has been constructed and the behind-the-scenes reading and analysis that underpins the statements (column 2). This opening section presents the reader with a summary overview of the current state of knowledge on the topic.

Example 5.1

A critical review

Taken from a paper on recycling by Smallbone (2005), this is an example of a good critical literature review put together with survey results to make policy recommendations.

The original text	**Deconstructing notes on the text**
The academic literature on pro-environmental behaviour and why people do and do not participate in recycling is extensive, but it is scattered in journals that range from those concerned with psychology through business, marketing and environmental science and sociology. It goes back to the 1970s, and by the mid 1980s a meta-analysis aiming to formulate a model of environmental behaviour could include 128 studies (Hines et al., 1986).	First sentence – tells me there is a lot of published material, and that contributions have been made from a variety of academic disciplines and perspectives. Second sentence – tells me how old the topic is and that there is already a meta-analysis of 128 studies, published in 1986.
Despite this effort, the results are frequently contradictory and are bedevilled by differences in local rubbish collection systems, variations in cultural expectations, and reliance on self-reported behaviour and small or biased samples, leaving a recent study to conclude that current knowledge on recycling behaviour is 'fragmented and inconclusive' (Davies et al., 2002: 54).	This is the summary analysis (an overall statement of 'what does this material tell us') and notes differences – reaffirming this opinion by citing a recent paper (at the time of writing her work).
Nevertheless it is possible to tease out a number of strands of thinking which together help to shed light on the validity of the three marketing assumptions described above.	Then she brings the paragraph back to her own research question.

Examine the paper again. You will see that Smallbone organises the material under three main headings (the framework):

- Targeting the green consumer using marketing communications.
- Green intentions and recycling behaviour.
- Could recycling become a social norm?

If we examine this structure further, we can see that each of these headings contains a varying number of paragraphs and references. This gives you an indication of how much material there was to review in total, and then how many authors had covered each theme. This information helps you, as a critical reader, to make judgements about the quantity of work reviewed and the relative importance of each topic.

- Targeting the green consumer using marketing communications – five paragraphs, covers 18 articles.
- Green intentions and recycling behaviour – three paragraphs, covers three articles.
- Could recycling become a social norm – three paragraphs, covers three articles.

Altogether, Smallbone has reviewed and analysed 24 papers.

So the critical dimension is achieved by reading the available material from a different perspective, looking at the topic through an alternative lens – the eyes of a marketing discipline. This is providing an alternative focus and that is one way that knowledge is advanced. Smallbone wants to make a point about the gap she found in the recycling knowledge and is using the literature to show that gap. In a policy-related context she wants to show that current policy may be focused on the wrong trajectory. Of course, she also wants to set the scene for future marketing campaigns.

Tip

See if you can apply an alternative discipline lens to the topic you are reviewing.

Example 5.2

Conceptual reviews

An example of conceptual review in an emerging field is Kindig's article, 'Understanding population health terminology' (2007). We suggest that you look up this article to get the most out of the discussion that follows.

We have to be sure that we are in agreement that the words we use have a shared meaning and understanding. Conceptual reviews are able to compare and contrast the different ways in which authors have used a specific word or concept. The following paragraph is my observation, not a reproduction of the original text. At first glance you might not think it is a review at all, but on closer reading of the original paper you will notice that Kindig (2007) is reviewing the state of knowledge on two concepts, which are often used in a confused way in public health discourse: public health and population health. So what makes this a conceptual review?

Kindig (2007) does not contain a methods section; neither does it state that it is a literature review, although it is. The context for the paper is the realisation that the different disciplines now contributing to the discourse on public health have different understandings and use of the core concepts. Now it is not just medicine that has an input, but also epidemiology, economics, sociology and psychology. Kindig defines and discusses many of the terms and concepts characterising this emerging field. This paper is written by an expert in the field, drawing on a wealth of personal and professional experience. The concepts are *public health*, an old term whose definition was once clear but is now becoming problematic, and *population health,* a relatively new term. In the final paragraph, Kindig gives his rationale for the study. This is a policy agenda and an important research question is proposed: 'What is the optimal balance of investments in the multiple determinants of health over the life course that will maximise overall health outcomes and minimise health inequalities at the population level?' Without an agreed definition of the core concepts the subsequent research will be of little use.

Kindig faced a similar problem that students have to face. There is a research question, but before you can begin to specify the research question and design the research methodology you have to be clear how the core concepts are understood and used (operationalised). Using Kindig (2007) as an example, this paper shows the complexity that might arise when examining current literature from a different paradigm or academic discipline.

Tip

Note down from each article you read how the core concepts have been used or operationalised. Are there different definitions in other disciplines and how has the definition changed over time?

Example 5.3

State-of-the-art reviews

We have selected a paper by Srivastava (2007) as an example of a state-of-the-art review. The paper is a comprehensive review of supply chain literature on green supply. (Srivastava, 2007). This is an expert review because the authors have developed an original framework through which to analyse the known body of work, as shown in the following quotation.

The paragraph below is based solely on the journal article abstract, using the original text. Note that the published review is described as 'comprehensive and all inclusive'. It must therefore have taken a long time to do. This paper does have a detailed methodological description. So what makes this a state-of-the-art review?

A perusal of the literature showed that a broad frame of reference for this subject is not adequately developed. A succinct classification is needed. The literature on green supply chain management is covered exhaustively from its conceptualisation, primarily taking a 'reverse logic angle'. This review classifies the problem context, on the methodological approach, maps mathematical tools and provides a timeline. (Srivastava, 2007: 53)

Example 5.4

Expert reviews

Ferlie is a well known expert on public policy. His review paper presents an overview of the organisational changes and management literature on recent large scale change within health care organisations. Ferlie notes that seven critics may argue that the approach adopted here is too subjective in orientation (Ferlie, 1997: 181). This example of a literature review is a self-declared subjective selection written by an expert on the topic of organisational and managerial change. It is therefore a traditional review, not a systematic review. Ferlie (1997), as an acknowledged expert, gives his opinion on the literature as it applies to health care. This following paragraph is my observation, not the original text. So what makes this an expert review?

> Ferlie (1997) explains his search and selection rationale. He observes that the subject matter is a diffuse field where the unit of analysis – organisational and managerial reform – is multifaceted. So, there is no conceptual consistency then. He observes that studies are based on diverse methodological and theoretical orientations, and randomised trials are rarely employed. Ferlie's search design consists of a two-stage model. The first stage involved a manual search of eight key journals known to the author. Ferlie traced earlier work by examining citations, and then selected those studies which *appeared to be of interest*. The second stage was the selection of a group of nine key texts which appeared to be of *particular interest*. The selected studies were chosen on the basis that:
>
> - they discuss organisational and managerial changes in health care at a macro rather than a micro level
> - they present primarily empirical data as well as interpretation
> - in the *judgement of the author,* they reflect the work of established scholars and research groups working in this field as indicated by professional reputation, citation and the winning of grants.

It is the description of the methodology that tells you that this is not a systematic review and that the author has used his expert knowledge to limit the search. An insight here is that by using citations and scanning key journals it is possible to identify a useful range of information. But it is the expertise that drives selection of material.

Tip

By scanning the citation list for each article you will quickly spot the key journals publishing material on your topic. It does not take long to identify them in the search stage as the same ones keep popping up. This will help to concentrate your search.

Example 5.5

Scoping reviews

Our example of a scoping review is a paper on the subject of firm acquisition by Barkema and Schijven (2008). As a reminder, a scoping review sets the scene for a future research agenda. This is my observation, not the original published text, on what makes this a scoping review.

> Barkema and Schijven (2008) provide an example of a critical literature review which summarises past research and presents a research agenda for the future. Barkema and Schijven set their review of firm acquisition in the contemporary management context at the time of writing. The consensus is that most acquisitions fail. Yet despite many academic insights into what needs to be done when acquiring a new company, the same mistakes appear to be repeated. Therefore, the authors note that *there is value in taking stock of past research and in outlining what remains to be explored and in drawing an agenda for future work* (2008: 595). There is a short methods section explaining what is covered in the review – studies published since 1980 in leading management journals plus some as yet unpublished work and work from other settings. The structure of the paper is balanced, consisting of 11 pages on the past review, six pages on the future agenda, together with summary tables of the selected papers. The summary tables are the evidence, presented to the reader.

The review documents what is already known. Then, using a critical analysis of the gaps in knowledge, it helps to refine the questions, concepts and theories and thus points the way to future research. It is also used as the first step in refining the questions for a subsequent systematic review. The pages of summary present the evidence to the reader, so that you can make your own assessment of the validity of the authors' claims.

So now you have looked at some published examples of different types of traditional critical reviews, this should help when you are reading for your own literature review and give you some ideas on how to get going.

Drawing up an analytical framework – how to sort the material

Although you might set out with a limited plan for the scope of your research, it can actually be a fluid and flexible process. The library search will show you the size of the body of work that exists. If you can't find anything, you may need to revise your research question or try alternative keywords. The advantage of a traditional review, which is less formally prescribed than a systematic review, is that you can add new thoughts and new themes to your plan throughout the process.

Figure 5.1 is a stylised presentation showing an overview of the typical process as straightforward and linear. Step 1 begins when you have obtained some papers, some information on theories and on the empirical applications of the theory. Step 2 is to read and begin to think what approach your critique will take. Make an analytical assessment of what you have in front of you. Step 3 is the point at which you can spot a knowledge gap.

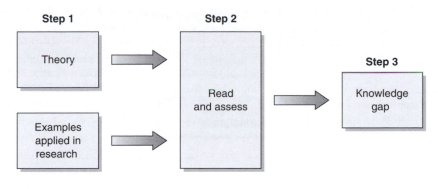

Figure 5.1   The analytical process

The review process

Figure 5.1 is an abstract representation. If we take a real-world example, you can see how this might begin to work out. Remember the Smallbone (2005) example covered 24 articles, so start this process as soon as you can. Begin to make notes, categorise your papers and start to write.

Mind map or table display of material

The assumption at this point is that you have printed off several articles and are ready to begin the next phase of analysis. One useful way to start is to lay out the material on your desk or on a big table, in bundles or piles. Figure 5.2 is based on an evaluation project where we needed to find out quickly how to evaluate a local Sure Start Partnership. Sure Start was a UK-government intervention in disadvantaged communities. The aim of the programme was to support parents of children under 5 years by bringing together all the statutory public and voluntary services working for families – thus forming a partnership. Over six months we had gathered together huge piles of paper, on a research question 'What is to be learned from Sure Start programme evaluations?' Figure 5.2 represents the desk display of the different materials that were obtained. Displaying the materials in this way helped us to conceptualise the topic and create a mind map. The skills you need to perform this task are 'differentiating' and 'categorising' your data.

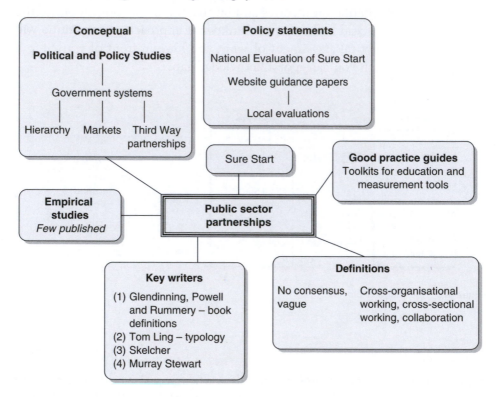

Figure 5.2   Example of a mind map/table sort of materials on Sure Start public partnership evaluation

This project was about public sector partnerships, so partnerships sit at the centre of the map. Both conceptual and empirical studies were retrieved – with some overlap; there were also government practice guidelines and public partnership evaluation toolkits. After skim reading all of this material we could confidently state that there was no clear definition of public partnership. There were several abstract models and public partnership evaluation toolkits, but few empirical examples of applying these models and none applying evaluation toolkits to local Sure Start interventions. This does not mean that there were none, just that we had not yet found them because they were not in the public domain.

Begin to categorise

So to recap. Step 1 begins when you have obtained some articles, possibly covering theories and some empirical applications of the theory. Step 2 is to read and begin to think what approach your critique will take, making an analytical assessment of what you have in front of you. Step 3 is to begin to categorise your material. The next section shows how you can take a single text and summarise the key points, authors, and concepts into a table.

Change management is a topical feature of modern management. The example on change management is summarised in Table 5.1. Shacklady-Smith (2006) advises her readers to be mindful of the historical, social, economic and political contexts when reviewing the change management literature. This is a useful example because it has several approaches, lots of empirical studies testing out the theory and a succinct critical summary and overview of the literature.

This is an example from a textbook, where the literature has already been summarised for you – remember, wherever possible you should attempt to consult the original publications to make up your own mind and develop your own critique. Nevertheless this type of review does serve as an introduction to help you get started and charts your 'enquiry chain' (O'Neill, 2005).

Table 5.1 Change management theory as a topic

Theoretical approaches	Relevant authors	How this differs
Mechanistic and planned	Lewin, 1958	Historical beginnings
Emergent process	Burnes, 1996	Challenges Lewin
Typologies of change:	Ackerman, 1997	Modern applications
Developmental		
Transitional		
Transformational		
How to change organisations	Empirical case studies	Applied to real situations

Source: Shacklady-Smith (2006:)

Moving to analysis and synthesis

So far this chapter has described different types of review and illustrated the types with published examples from a range of topics. This was followed by some advice on how to begin making sense of the literature you are reading.

In his classic text *Doing a Literature Review*, Hart (1998) has given us a checklist of the types of question you might use to interrogate an article and which will also provide a framework for your write-up:

- What are the key sources?
- What are the key theories, concepts and ideas?
- What are the key epistemological and ontological grounds for the discipline?
- What are the main questions and problems that have been addressed to date?
- How has knowledge in the topic been structured and organised?
- How have approaches to these questions increased our understanding and knowledge?
- What are the origins and definitions of the topic?
- What are the major issues and debates about the topic?

You will find your own preferred way of beginning to put information together. The process of searching, reading, then refining the scope and re-searching is a cyclical process. It is unlikely that you will do each of these activities once only. By now you will have explored several sources and articles, maybe even different sorts of literature, you will know the key issues and have found a focus for your review. Next, you have to concentrate on documenting the themes, similarities and differences in the literature you are reviewing. Synthesise on a thematic basis, so the evidence from single studies is pooled. This takes us to the next three steps towards analysis.

Stage 1

Write a summary of the important parts of each paper; take three papers to begin with. You will start, with three sets of information and two or three themes (which might include theory, results or data analysis). Look again at Example 5.1 where Smallbone (2005) stated the three key topic areas the literature review covered. Evaluate the evidence that is presented, question for yourself how valid and reliable the evidence is. This is easier to do if you already have knowledge of one subject area and can apply it to a different discipline or a different focus, as Smallbone did with marketing and recycling. At this stage you are writing descriptively – it is just a summary. Later you will expand on the number of papers you review and build up the evidence, and maybe revise your themes as you go along.

Stage 2

Now compare and contrast the three papers and themes: what is the same, what is similar, what is different? Write short summary paragraphs of the key points you want to make, drawing from each of the three individual extracts you produced in step 1. Now you should have one comparative set of information but it is no longer in a bibliographic format but combined. Be careful with time sequences – analyse the work in a chronological order. If it is a new subject area for you, question the plausibility. Does what you read make sense from your own experience? You may be the person who makes a critical challenge to longstanding ideas or theory. At this stage you are writing critically.

Stage 3

This is a cyclical process. You will read more, make more notes, and discard some notes, read and review, write, read, review. Build up your case now. It is important to document the good and negative or weak features, the strengths and limitations of the method as well as the explanatory arguments. Keep returning to your original research question, aim and objectives to make sure what you are writing is still relevant. Some students get to this point and change direction because an in-depth understanding of the problem helps them to refocus on the research problem.

Tip

When writing, check the words at the beginning of each paragraph. If each paragraph begins with an author's name then maybe you still have a format that is based on description, where each source of information is presented independently one after the other. Now repeat this test with each sentence. Try not to begin every sentence or paragraph with the author's name.

The presentation of your review

The aim of a traditional narrative literature review is to provide a critical review, not a description, a catalogue or shopping list. It is a new picture or story you are presenting, with your judgements made from a sound basis of evidence, reflection and sometimes experience.

Make sure that you summarise current knowledge in a clear and consistent logical way. Think of your review as a story, with an introduction, middle and end. The format could be like this:

- Introduction – guide the reader through. Give an overview of what is known and how you will present your critique – the trailer. Make the purpose clear from the start, explain the structure.
- Method – this is optional but it does help the reader to see how and from where you have obtained your information. You can also state here possible themes/issues that you have decided not to include.
- Theme 1.
- Theme 2.

- Theme 3.
- Discussion and critical summary paragraphs.
- Conclusion – states what your contribution to the debate is. Show the gap. Do not introduce new material. If relevant, how does it link into your research project?

Summarising the gap – dare to have an opinion

You need to convince the reader that you are fully conversant with the current debate on your topic, that you know who the key writers are and the ideological agendas or perspectives from which they work. You want to be original and show how your analysis and synthesis brings insights or a new dimension to the topic. Finally, show that you have identified the knowledge gap, especially if the purpose of the review is scoping to set up a research project. Highlight any consensus, any exceptions to that consensus, and note the methodological or theoretical limitations in the work you have reviewed.

─────────────────── Summary ───────────────────

This chapter has tried to tease out the different types of traditional literature review that you may encounter in your reading. Tell the reader what the purpose of your review is and what type of review it is. The traditional review is flexible. It allows us to use different types of evidence, draw on quantitative and qualitative work, on research and non-research materials. A final point is to remind you to be self-aware, reflective and critical. It remains the key research method that all students have to undertake at some point in their academic career. It does not have to be labour intensive, and can be done within the budget and time constraints of a student project. It is the first step you need to undertake before you can begin a systematic review.

In Chapter 7 we cover systematic review. To aspire to the systematic review as the gold standard is good, but first you have to know how to do an effective traditional review. Systematic reviews, if done properly, are time-consuming, expensive and are usually undertaken by a team of research assistants and researchers. Researchers who produce systematic reviews have to have an overview of the current literature. In effect, they have insights from a scoping review to formulate or modify the research question, before they can apply the specific research question and designate the inclusion and exclusion criteria.

6

WRITING UP YOUR REVIEW

Key Points

- A good review is more than a description, it critically compares and contrasts
- A good review is original, perceptive and analytical
- A good review is based on a fair (unbiased) selection of sources
- A good review identifies the knowledge gaps

Be aware

- A good review is not a descriptive list
- A good review is not a book-by-book, article-by-article summary
- A good review is not an annotated bibliography or a simple write-up of statements describing the information in each article
- A good review is not a series of paragraphs describing each source separately
- A good review is not regurgitating the findings by stringing quotes from several sources.
- A good review is not presented in alphabetical order

Overview

To recap, where are we now? In Chapter 5 we established a number of reasons for undertaking a review. We described a traditional review as a comprehensive review which summarises past research and draws conclusions. The traditional review can take many forms. Depending on the purpose of the review, it is usually critical, but it may also be a conceptual review, a state-of-the-art review, an expert review or a scoping review. We emphasised that a good review must be more than descriptive: it should be original, perceptive, and analytical, based on a fair selection of sources. Then the critical comparison and contrasting of ideas and evidence leads into the gap of what still needs to be known and researched. So now, in Chapter 6, we give you more guidance and advice on how to avoid some of the most common pitfalls made by those new to academic writing and discussion in compiling a traditional review. First, let's think about some key formats that you will encounter – the abstract, the summary and an annotated bibliography.

During your research methodology training you will be exposed to several research methods textbooks. When we began teaching critical literature review to postgraduate students ten years ago it was noticeable that at that time very few authors included a chapter on review, and even when they did the body of material consisted mainly of descriptions of the search and assessments of various types of evidence (for example, Bryman, 2004). These days, possibly as a result of the growing interest in systematic review (see Chapter 7), more has been written. But there still remains a gap in textbooks on guidance in putting the material together and writing the review. So, in this chapter, we draw on some published work and student reviews to illustrate what to do and what to avoid.

There are two ways, or formats, of presenting your review, depending on the context:

1 A short summary.
2 A self-standing review.

It is the latter that will form the majority of guidance in this chapter.

A short summary

The simplest format of review is a summary of the relevant literature. This format is often found as an introduction to an article that is presenting a new empirical study. Depending on the journal and traditions of the discipline, the scope of this example of a review is typically very short and narrow. Another way to describe this format is as a fact-building approach, which can be labelled 'stringing' or, by Metcalfe (2003), as the 'dump' method.

Stringing or the dump method

Essentially, this short summary review is 'stringing'. I have called this 'stringing' because you string together a range of work into two or three paragraphs but without actually developing the material, describing the context or comparing or contrasting the findings. This format is used specifically when several references support a statement or when a topic or issue has been explored by a number of authors.

Example 6.1

Stringing

This is a paragraph taken from a report on pharmacy practice research. The paragraph from Wilson and Jesson (2003) summarises in six lines *some* of the key articles covering ways of improving repeat prescribing:

> A variety of methods have been used, including visits of community pharmacists to GPs to discuss prescribing in specific therapeutic areas (NPC and NHSE, 1998), review of patient records by pharmacists (Sykes et al., 1996; Goldstein et al., 1997; Granas and Bates, 1999) and clinical medication reviews at the practice or patient's home (Burtonwood et al., 1998; Mackie et al., 1999; Krska et al., 2000; Zermansky et al., 2001). (Wilson and Jesson, 2003: 225)

You will observe that there is very little detail of the context or content of the articles referenced. There is a very sweeping, generalised statement followed by a list of references. The reader has to do the work, the writers assume that they are speaking to an informed audience who are familiar with the topic and know the authors and references, or they will follow up the references. This type of summary is typical of journals that have a 3,000 word limit.

Tip

Look for yourself and see whether this is a feature in your discipline. When you have obtained two or three published articles begin with the literature review, usually at the beginning of an article, and see whether the author has given sufficient information. To follow up key articles is a good starting point if you are new to the topic.

The following sentence is taken from the first draft of a student review:

> Recycling is a premier example of the collective coproduction of a local government program (Brudney 1990; Brudney and England 1983; Ferris 1984, 1988; Sundeen 1998).

This stringing sentence tells the reader that the following authors have made some observation about recycling and local government and that this is a long-standing phenomenon covering the period 1983–1998. If you are going to use stringing sentences, then the presentation can be improved by putting the dates in chronological rather than alphabetical order:

> Recycling is a premier example of the collective coproduction of a local government program (Brudney and England, 1983; Ferris, 1984, 1988; Brudney, 1990; Sundeen, 1998).

Tip

When you write your review, pay attention to the referencing format required by your institution.

A self-standing review

Next, we will consider a self standing review, by which we mean a complete review that goes into more detail than an abstract and is a coherent body of work in its own right. We assume that you will be writing in greater detail than in a summary stringing review. Different disciplines have different expectations about the format that a traditional review will take. However, we have found the following advice to be useful with our students.

Structure and writing up

The traditional review is presented like any other essay. That is: with an Abstract or Summary, Introduction, Middle (main body divided into sub-topics), and a Conclusion, as shown in Table 6.1. This formula may vary depending on your subject and discipline. Always check with your supervisor what the requirements are. For example, rather than a short 350-word abstract, you may be asked to write an extended abstract or even an executive summary. The right-hand column in Table 6.1 offers a suggestion on length, but this is a very personal and contextual issue that you have to decide for yourself. If you have a mature topic or type of knowledge, then the number of articles will be large and your review could be lengthy, whereas there will be fewer published materials on an emerging issue and therefore it could be a short review.

It is not necessary to copy out all the methodological details of each study – you have given a reference so the reader can do that if it is relevant – but what we need to know are the key points and that depends on the framework and focus of your research question. What you impart to the reader has to reinforce your argument. For instance, if the article you are reviewing is an empirical

Table 6.1 The structure of a traditional narrative literature review

Section	Contents	Suggested length
Abstract	A succinct summary of the whole review	Up to 350 words
Introduction	What is the basic aim, goal of the review? Why is the subject of interest? What is the scale and scope of the review? What is included and excluded? What are the focus, basic definitions and concepts? Is it a mature or emerging topic? Explain the organisation of the review – sequence of themes. Trailer – what will follow?	2–3 lines per sentence 3 sentences per paragraph Each paragraph has a new topic From 3–6 paragraphs expect to cover 3–6 topics
Main body Sub-topics Link paragraphs together by the first and last sentences	This section depends on your topic. These are just suggestions: (a) Methodological frameworks (b) Conceptual evolution (c) Theme 1 (d) Theme 2 (e) Theme 3 Is your discussion within each theme or do you need additional discussion paragraphs to bring the work together?	3 sentences per paragraph
Conclusion The gap	Relate back to the introduction, purpose, aim and objectives Summarise the important aspects in the review Evaluate the current state of the literature Identify flaws or gaps in existing knowledge Outline areas for future research Lead into your research proposal	From 3–6 paragraphs 3 sentences per paragraph

research study, what is it about the design, sampling, data collection, analysis or conclusion that are noteworthy? Obviously, if the articles under review are policy papers or theoretical conceptual papers, then the approach will be different.

Abstract, executive summary and annotated bibliography

This section tells you what an abstract is. It tells you how to write an abstract and shows how abstracts are collated to form an annotated bibliography. It is important to differentiate between an abstract, an annotated bibliography and a review. Avoid using abstracts as your sole source of information; always check with the complete article.

What is an abstract?

An abstract is a short summary of an academic paper. Abstracts are important for three reasons:

1 They help you to undertake the search for literature (see Chapter 2) because databases will show you an abstract of the whole article.
2 They help you to make your decision on whether the article is relevant to your review
3 They are a model in that they show you how to write your own.

The reason abstracts are raised here is that some of those new to academic writing produce a literature review which reads like a series of abstracts. There is one paragraph for each article, but this format is never followed through to the next analytical stage of providing a critical comparison. There is no common theme or argument running through or linking the abstracts. Abstracts are purely condensed, succinct, descriptive summaries found at the beginning of a scholarly journal or in periodical indexes.

By comparison, when you write an abstract for your own review, the abstract should be able to stand on its own. The format for writing an abstract varies (see Table 6.2). Based on journal requirements, they can be either structured or flexible.

Table 6.2 Examples of some journal abstract formats

Journal	Abstract requirements
Medical journals	Introduction
	Method
	Results
	Discussion
Emerald Journals, e.g. *European Journal of Marketing*	Purpose
	Design/methodological approach
	Findings
	Research limitations/implications
	Practical implications
	Originality/value
	Keywords
	Paper type
	Maximum 250 words
Resources, Conservation and Recycling	Not structured. A succinct abstract of no more than 300 words, clearly describing the entire paper

---
Tip

Emeraldinsight have published a really useful guide, *How to ... write an abstract* (Elsevier, 2008).

In their instructions for authors, journals usually specify the number of words allowed for an abstract and for the article. You are allowed typically no more than 500 words for an abstract. If you are not writing for a journal but for an academic dissertation, then you will write a summary. Try to summarise your work on to one page – this is your version of an abstract.

There are two important points to remember about abstracts:

1 Do not rely on a journal abstract only when researching a topic. Obtain the original and make your own evaluation of the work.
2 Do not write sentences in your review based solely on an abstract.

Executive summary

An executive summary is not an abstract. It is a summation of the key findings, implications and recommendations of a report. The executive summary usually appears at the front of a report. The styles of writing and contents vary. Sometimes there can be up to four pages summarising the aim, objectives, context, methods and results. Quite often, however, the key findings and implications only are provided, in which case the reader has to read the complete report to find out other details.

Annotated bibliography

Another error new writers might make when writing up a traditional narrative review is to write a series of paragraphs, or abstracts, which read like an annotated bibliography. An annotated bibliography is really a series of notes about other articles. The purpose of an annotated bibliography is to present an overview of the published literature on a topic by summarising the key articles. Olin and Uris libraries (2008) offers practical advice on preparing an annotated bibliography.

An annotated bibliography is a list of citations to books, articles and documents. Each citation is followed by a brief (usually about 150 words) descriptive and evaluative paragraph, the annotation. The purpose of the annotation is to inform the reader of the relevance, accuracy and quality of the sources cited. The annotation is a concise and succinct analysis. (Olin and Uris libraries, 2008)

To write an annotated bibliography you need to summarise each article briefly. Be careful not to confuse an annotated bibliography with a bibliographic database, as described in Chapter 2. There are various kinds of annotated bibliography. Most annotated bibliographies include an introduction, which sets out the purpose of the review and a methods section, which describes the selection of sources cited. Table 6.3 lists three reviews, comparing the purpose and presentational approach of the results.

Table 6.3 Selected annotated bibliographies

Annotated bibliography	Purpose	Organising structure
Macinko and Starfield (2002)	To present an overview of the published literature on equity in health and to summarise key articles relevant to the mission of the International Society for Equity in Health.	Authors provide short summaries of examples of different approaches to studying health equity, rather than providing an exhaustive list of equity-related articles. The articles are subdivided into four categories. The reviews are one or two paragraphs in length.
Ceglowski and Bacigalupa (2002)	To update an earlier review on childcare research undertaken in 1987.	The review is organised in four sections, covering the same questions as those asked in 1987. Results are presented in tabular format, with references beneath each table.
Kendall et al. (2009)	First, to present a comprehensive list of sports scheduling papers, to serve as a starting point for those requiring information and to those wishing to update their knowledge. Second, to present the methodologies that have been used in solving these types of problem.	Articles are numbered 1 to 162 and organised in four sections. The summaries are one or two sentences in length.

Tip

You will probably begin your review by writing in an annotated bibliographic format. Resist the temptation, but if you cannot, then you have to move on to stage 2 – integrating.

Task

Look at some other annotated bibliographies. Two examples from the subject of marketing are: 'Studies of negative political advertising: an annotated bibliography' (Hartman, 2000) and 'Towards effective poster presentations: an annotated bibliography' (Brownlie, 2007). Note that there is no summary discussion or conclusion to an annotated bibliography.

If you stop writing at this point you have only done half a review. An 'ordinary' review can often be descriptive and mechanical, whereby the writer simply summarises the information from a range of documents in chronological or alphabetical order. *This format does not get you high marks.* A literature review should *not* be merely a list describing or summarising one article after another. It has to be discursive, analysed prose. The reader wants to gain more from reading your review, to understand more, than a simple list or 'string' of previous publications would provide. So we are looking for not an annotated bibliography but an argued analytical review.

Writing the review

An analytical framework

The review must have a guiding aim or goal. What is the research question? How does the review inform the research question? What is the purpose, scope, length of the review? You must tell the reader what ideas and knowledge are established because it sets the scope of the review and helps them decide whether the review will be useful.

You organise the review into sections that present themes or theory based on what you are looking for in each article.

Move forward in a chronological order, from the oldest articles first, and then show to what extent later research *confirms* or *refutes* those earlier studies. That is how the review develops these ideas.

In Example 6.2, Tuch and O'Sullivan (2007) present a review of empirical research on the impact of acquisitions on firm performance. They have pre-understanding. That means they are already familiar with the literature and they already have a good idea of the body of knowledge, but they want to bring it together in a comprehensive review. Their hypothesis is that, in practice, the promised gains are not easily identified. They state that the search has been limited to studies in accounting and finance – thus setting the selective paradigm from which the evidence will be collated. Example 6.2 shows the organisational structure of the article – in six sections.

Example 6.2

Acquisitions

This example shows the analytical framework for the review. The words in italics are from the original. The topic is the impact of acquisitions on firm performance: a review of the evidence (Tuch and O'Sullivan, 2007).

Framework of the original paper	Comment on content or purpose of each section
Introduction Includes an overview of the topic. The purpose of the article. Description of the methodological approach – what is covered and excluded.	The introduction sets up the story for the reader. The description of the method serves as a trailer for what follows – introducing the key themes
A Review of Acquirer Performance *Evidence from Event Study Research* *Short-run event studies, Long-run event studies* *Evidence from Accounting Research*	Main heading Three subheaded sections Within each section the perceived weaknesses of the methodology are discussed
The Impact of Bid Characteristics on Performance *The mood of acquisition* *Method of payment* *Relative size of target and bidder* *Industrial relatedness of the bidder and target*	Main heading Four subheaded sections
The Role of Pre-bid Performance	
Discussion **Conclusion**	

This example on mergers and acquisition is a traditional review because the style of review and the presentation of the analysis are based on the authors' pre-understanding of the current literature. It is not a systematic review because it has not followed the systematic review methodology. Authors have selected material to include and made decisions on what to exclude, but the basis of this decision process is not clear. The article demonstrates a higher level of integrating the information than a shopping list of articles, whether in alphabetical or chronological order. By setting up themes, the authors produce a more comprehensive *analysis* of the contents than is possible in the annotated bibliography format. There is a flow of ideas which combines several sources, reinforcing the importance of each idea. The reader therefore gains a much better understanding based on the authors' opinions.

Key words or phrases to help you move from stage 1 to stage 2

So far in this chapter we have explained the purpose of different short summaries of literature. We assume that you are now ready to move on to writing a more comprehensive version of your review. At this stage, you have decided on your selection of articles to review, drawn up an analytical framework and now you have to start writing.

Choosing a good writing style

A good approach to writing is to list article you have read. Table 6.4 shows how the beginning of each sentence looks to the reader. What this tells the reader is that what follows is likely to be based on a summary paragraph only.

Table 6.4 Writing styles – opening sentence (note the date order)

Good opening style	Opening style to avoid
Early work by Thomas (1996) shows that...	Thomas (1996) said...
Another study on the topic by Brown (2000) asserts that...	Brown said (2000)...
The latest research (Smith, 2003) shows...	Smith (2003) wrote...

However, beginning every paragraph with the authors' names is not a good review – it is a bibliography list. You have to juxtapose and link ideas. Be critical, be comparative. Below is some guidance on how to write an argued, critical sentence. Example 6.3 is taken from a Masters-level research proposal. The paragraph summarises three sources of financial performance measurement literature.

Example 6.3

Masters-level review, using a comparative style

This section will analyse the traditional performance measurement systems, which according to Broadbent (1999) are bound up with the manner in which financial reports have evolved. As Brignall (1998: xxx) identified, 'the measurement of financial performance is intended to ensure the attainment of an organisation's financial objectives: the focus of budgetary control'. Also, as Johnson and Clark (2002) added, financial measures are easy to apply and understand and, most importantly, they allow for both internal and external benchmarking. Moreover, as Whiting (1986) noted, financial measures allow a company's stakeholders to measure its performance in an easily comparable manner.

1 The first sentence is the trailer, telling the reader what follows and noting the context of performance measurement.
2 Each source used is a textbook.
3 Instead of beginning each sentence with: Brignell..., Johnson and Clark..., Whiting..., the author has used comparative devices to enhance the readability:

As Brignell identified...,
Also, as Johnson and Clark added...
Moreover, as Whiting noted...

Tip

Avoid writing words such as 'Brown *thinks*...' or 'Smith *feels*...' It is better to write 'Brown *discusses*...' , 'Brown *argues*...', or 'Brown *considers*...'.

To help develop a critical analytical approach you can group sources together by using connecting, linking words such as: *also, additionally, again, similarly, a similar opinion.* Alternatively, you can group contrasting ideas together, using words such as *however, conversely, on the other hand, nevertheless, a contrasting opinion, a different approach.* The use of an approach that links ideas is also a device to avoid starting every sentence with an author's name! When you report on the ideas or arguments proposed by an author, use words such as '*According to Smith...*' or 'as *Brown argues convincingly*', or '*the author states...*'. Table 6.5 sets out a list of synonyms, which are alternative words or verbs for saying something similar, that you might find useful.

Table 6.5 Verbs and synonyms, to use in writing about text and making an argument

Account for	Clarify	Describe	Exemplify	Investigate	Recognise
Analyse	Compare and contrast	Determine	Expand	Judge	Reflect
Argues	Conclude	Discuss	Explain	Justify	Refer to
Assess	Criticise	Distinguish	Exhibit	Narrate	Relate to
	Debate	Differentiate	Identify	Outline	Report
Assert	Defend	Evaluate	Illustrate	Persuade	Review
Assume	Define	Emphasise	Imply	Propose	Suggest
Claim	Demonstrate	Examine	Indicate	Question	Summarise

However, some may or may not be appropriate, depending on the context of your review.

Browne and Keeley (2004) have compiled a useful checklist to use when developing critical reading skills. The words or phrases listed in Table 6.6 can equally be applied to critical writing.

Table 6.6 Forming critical sentences using signalling words

As a consequence of *x* then *y*
Consequently, ...
Hence ...
Therefore, ...
Thus ...
In short ...
In effect ... / It follows that ...
This indicates that ...
This suggests that ...
It should be clear now that ... / The point I am making is ...
This points to the conclusion that ...
The most obvious explanation is ...
This means that ...
Finally, ...

Source: Brown and Keeley (2004)

Making an argument within the context of critical writing means presenting reasons to support your point of view. An argument includes:

- outlining a position or point of view
- attempting to persuade others to accept your point of view
- giving reasons to support your view.

A good review can be improved by adding 'transition statements'. This means using signalling language to inform the reader which direction the review is taking.

The 'so what?' question, originality and making a value judgement

The literature review needs to flow. It should not be an aimless description of unlinked theories and ideas. Try to link up each paragraph with the next one. At the end of the review ask yourself 'so what?' This will take you on to the summary and conclusion.

Most reviews will present their ideas for future research, which is 'the gap' in knowledge. Returning to Example 6.2, Tuch and O'Sullivan (2007) make several suggestions in their conclusion, but to note just three here:

1 To examine the relationship between the monitoring potential of acquiring boards and subsequent performance.
2 To research the decision-making and monitoring of the board in takeover bids.
3 To undertake a comprehensive analysis of the performance implications of failed bids, incorporating the reasons for failures.

Summary

Chapters 5 and 6 should be read as a package because they concentrate on how to undertake a traditional literature review. Chapter 5 showed you the various types of traditional review that you might encounter: critical, conceptual, state-of-the-art, expert and scoping reviews. Each one serves a different purpose and often can stand alone as a form of review.

Chapter 6 continued the work on traditional literature review by drawing attention to more formats and concepts that you will encounter. Writing an abstract is probably the final act before completing your review, but this advice is given early because we would prefer that you do not rely solely on published abstracts as a basis for your review. It is important to know the difference between an annotated bibliography and a literature review because of the temptation to write a review that looks like an annotated bibliography. Finally, you can improve your writing and make it more critical by using keywords that force you to rearrange the structure of each sentence and paragraph. Chapters 7 and 8 describe the process required for undertaking a systematic review. If you are undertaking a traditional review you may want to go straight to Chapter 9 to revise referencing styles.

7

THE SYSTEMATIC REVIEW

Key points

- To undertake a systematic review you need some working knowledge and understanding of the field
- Systematic review uses a standardised, structured, protocol-driven methodology
- The methodology is focused, explicit and must be transparent
- Systematic review requires a rigorous, systematic, comprehensive and exhaustive search for *all* the relevant literature
- Systematic review claims to be objective, balanced and unbiased

Be aware

- Systematic review methodology may not be appropriate for undergraduate-level reviews
- Systematic review is time-consuming and can be expensive
- Systematic reviews are usually undertaken by more than one person; they are usually a team effort, to do the scanning, screening and quality assessment to reduce bias
- Systematic review is dependent on access to electronic databases and a range of available databases and can therefore be limited by the effectiveness of the databases
- Systematic review is typically restricted to published, peer-reviewed, academic work

---

Overview

Literature reviews can be envisaged as a continuum, ranging from traditional review to systematic review.

Traditional review ——————————— Systematic review
No defined method ——————————— Rigorous method
Exploratory/creative ——————————— Transparent/replicable

This chapter begins by describing the context in which systematic review has developed as a methodology in evidence-based practice. It then takes you step by step through the explicit stages of the methodology, as shown in Figure 7.1. You will learn how to develop your review protocol and the importance of documenting every stage of the process. The chapter ends with some examples of more sophisticated and complex reviews.

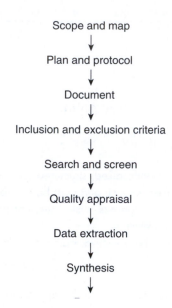

Scope and map
↓
Plan and protocol
↓
Document
↓
Inclusion and exclusion criteria
↓
Search and screen
↓
Quality appraisal
↓
Data extraction
↓
Synthesis
↓

Figure 7.1   Key stages in a systematic review

Definitions

Systematic review

The term, or concept, systematic review is used in two ways: it can refer to the prescribed methodology (a means – method) or to the output report itself (a report). This first definition, by Sweet and Moynihan (2007: 1), written with a healthcare context in mind, encapsulates all the key buzzwords which define a systematic review:

> Systematic reviews provide a systematic, transparent *means* for gathering, synthesising and appraising the findings of studies on a particular topic or question. The aim is to minimise the bias associated with single studies and non systematic reviews. (our italics)

Or it describes the output:

> A systematic review is a *research article* that identifies relevant studies, appraises their quality and summarises their results using scientific methodology. (Kahn et al., 2003: 1, our italics)

Identifying and sifting through all the relevant studies and evaluating each according to predefined criteria is what distinguishes a systematic review from a traditional review. Table 7.1 sets out the key differences.

Table 7.1 Comparative table of scoping review and systematic review

	Traditional (scoping) review	Systematic review
Aim	To gain a broad understanding, and description of the field	Tightly specified aim and objectives with a specific review question
Scope	Big picture	Narrow focus
Planning the review	No defined path, allows for creativity and exploration	Transparent process and documented audit trail
Identifying studies	Searching is probing, moving from one study to another, following up leads	Rigorous and comprehensive search for ALL studies
Selection of studies	Purposive selection made by the reviewer	Predetermined criteria for including and excluding studies
Quality assessment	Based on the reviewer's opinion	Checklists to assess the methodological quality of studies
Analysis and synthesis	Discursive	In tabular format and short summary answers
Methodological report	Not necessarily given	Must be presented for transparency

Source: Adapted from Pilbean and Denyer (2008)

Task

Go to the internet and enter the keywords: 'traditional literature review' and then 'systematic literature review' in the search box. Note the difference in the number of hits your search engine throws up.

The sheer volume of new research studies published these days makes it hard for researchers, practitioners and policy makers to know what is currently useful. This is a knowledge management problem and the aim of systematic reviews is to help bring this problem under control. For practitioners, the limitations of acting on single case study articles is that they may misrepresent the balance of available research evidence. In addition, studies can be of variable quality in terms of their design, execution, analysis and reporting. Moreover, research reports can be biased.

Systematic review for clinical biomedical research was formalised over 20 years ago in the UK through the Cochrane Collaborative, but since then it has been adopted worldwide and to some extent by most other fields of research. The purpose is to combine information from various sources to provide more data to answer a specified research question *without the need to set up a new study*. The Cochrane papers provide a valuable resource and guidance to practitioners and students undertaking a systematic review. These reviews adopt a strict scientific methodology, as shown in Table 7.2, which may not be appropriate for your student subject or topic. It is best to check with your supervisor which type of review you should undertake.

Evidence-based practice

Evidence-based policy or practice (EBP) began in healthcare research, in medicine and nursing, but it is now to be found in other areas, such as education, the probation service, regeneration policy and practice, housing, social care and criminal justice. You will notice from this list that in the UK these are all public services, where a large body of research is commissioned regularly, so there is ample material to review.

Several research centres, based in academic institutions, have been set up to collate the evidence and to help researchers adapt the Cochrane guidelines by producing specialised guidelines and toolkits. Some of these are listed in Appendix 3. For example, in social care, the Social Care Institute for Excellence (SCIE) sets its own framework for systematic reviews which covers five domains: policy knowledge, organisational knowledge, practitioner knowledge, user knowledge and research knowledge. The SCIE quality agenda covers empirical evidence of policy and practice, including the use of testimony from users and carers, a field which would not be highly rated in other subject contexts.

As we noted earlier, some authors argue that systematic review is a 'better' research method than traditional review because it is a more rigorous and therefore 'scientific' approach to the practice of literature reviewing (see Torgerson (2003) on education research and Petticrew and Roberts (2006) on the social sciences). Rigorous and scientific, in this context, refers to the systematic protocol methodology, compared to the looser and more flexible approach implicit in the traditional review. However, there is rather less consensus in the social science disciplines as to what constitutes evidence and appropriate methodological paradigms, each academic field having its own preferences.

Business and management research

The development of evidence-based management and the practice of undertaking systematic reviews in the business and management field has been slow. The problems for business and management subjects has been well articulated by Tranfield et al. (2003: 208). However, it should be acknowledged that the business and management field covers a diverse range of subjects, including marketing, finance and accounting, work organisation and psychology, economics and international business, each of which has its own research paradigm and acceptable approaches to research. Thus it can be difficult to impose the systematic review methodology on to their work. To meet this challenge the Advanced Institute of Management Research (AIM) researchers at Cranfield University have developed a training package to encourage the use of systematic review in business schools (Pilbean and Denyer, 2007/8). Tranfield et al. (2003) argue convincingly that, compared with the medical and biological sciences, there are significant onto-logical, epistemological and methodological differences in the many disciplines which go under the 'management' umbrella, and this makes it even more problematic to adopt wholesale the prescribed approach to systematic review.

Social science and cross-disciplinary systematic reviews

Other authors have noted that the systematic review methodology has not always been successful in social science and multidisciplinary research. A really interesting discussion on the limitations of a protocol-driven methodology is to be found in a systematic review which set out to answer this question: *What empirical evidence is available on the relationships between mental health problems and social exclusion?* (Curran et al., 2007). This study had to combine the literature covering two top-ics: health (mental health problems) and social policy (social exclusion). Both of these concepts are subject to varying usage over time and place. The authors of this review noted other challenges arose because much of the work was located in grey literature, such as in policy documents and government reports, or research from major charities or think tanks. The conclusion, in the context of trying to apply the systematic protocol to social science and cross-disciplinary research, was:

> There are a number of challenges to be overcome: poorly defined topics; inconsistent use of key words and controlled vocabulary; abstracts that do not effectively com-municate the content of the paper or are not accessible in bibliographic databases and resource and technology problems. (Curran et al., 2007: 305)

The observations made about business and management research and social science and cross-disciplinary systematic reviews are here to illustrate some of the hazards implicit in taking a methodology from its original discipline – medicine and healthcare – and adapting it to other disciplines.

A half-way review – rapid appraisal

So what are we saying here? We argue in this book that a systematic review actually builds on a traditional, critical or scoping review, as described in Chapters 5 and 6, but there are two main differences: the *reason* for undertaking a review and the *manner* of performing a review.

- A systematic review is a comprehensive review of *all* published articles selected to address a specific question using a systematic method of identifying relevant studies in order to minimise biases and error.
- The details of the approach used in a systematic review must be documented in the methods section of the review report.
- Systematic reviews have a structured methodology which must be transparent to its readers.
- The starting point is having a key specific question to answer.
- The whole process is summarised in Table 7.2.

Table 7.2   The key phases of a systematic review

Phase 1: Mapping the field through a scoping review.   What do we know and what are the knowledge gaps (as described in Chapter 5). How much relevant material is available?

Prepare the review plan. This includes the method and the protocol for the systematic review. Define the question or questions, compile key words. Set up the inclusion and exclusion criteria. Design the data extraction pro-forma or data sheet.

Phase 2: Comprehensive search.   Access the electronic databases and search using your key words. Search and document the search results.

Check whether the hits are relevant or are you coming up with too many hits. If so, do you need to refine the search and revise the key words? Do you need to revise the inclusion and exclusion criteria? Do you need to change the research question being addressed? Document the results/ numbers in a table. Screen the title, the abstract and, if relevant, print or obtain the paper.

Phase 3: Quality assessment.   Read the full paper and apply the quality assessment, using the 'hierarchy of research'. Decide whether papers are IN or OUT of your review. Document the reasons for excluding papers and compile a numerical table of the process.

Phase 4: Data extraction.   Write down the relevant data on to your pre-designed extraction sheet. This can be handwritten or in an electronic format.

Phase 5: Synthesis.   Synthesise the data from each individual article into one. Shows what we know now and what we still need to know. Is a meta-analysis or a mathematical synthesis feasible?

Phase 6: Write up.   Write up a balanced, impartial and comprehensive report, using a systematic review format, presenting the process reports which will enable another researcher to replicate your review. Disseminate to inform practice.

One of the limitations of the systematic methodology is that to do a good systematic review takes time, resources and ideally more than one researcher. You will note that most published systematic reviews are multi-authored. That should not automatically deter you from doing your review using the systematic methodology, but you do need to recognise and note the limitations. This methodology is more appropriate for Masters-level and doctoral work. Such a review might be called a rapid review. In the professional sphere, 'rapid appraisals' are reviews of existing evidence which are not fully developed systematic reviews. They are descriptive and can be completed in 8–12 weeks, as advised by the Government Social Research Unit (GSRU):

Rapid evidence appraisals collate descriptive outlines of the available evidence on a topic, critically appraise them (including an economic appraisal), sift out studies of poor quality and provide an overview of what that evidence is telling us and what is missing from it. (GSR, 2008: 12)

The GSR process is based on a fairly comprehensive electronic search, which can include some print materials, but it does not involve an exhaustive search.

Development of the review protocol

In Chapter 5 we described the key features of traditional review and in Chapter 6 we gave more guidance on writing up your review. So at this stage we assume that you have undertaken a traditional review. Use the checklist by Hart (1998) and map your findings:

- What are the key sources?
- What are the key theories, concepts and ideas?
- What are the key epistemological and ontological grounds for the discipline?
- What are the main questions and problems that have been addressed to date?
- How has knowledge in the topic been structured and organised?
- How have approaches to these questions increased our understanding and knowledge?
- What are the origins and definitions of the topic?
- What are the major issues and debates about the topic?

Figure 7.2 shows the simple mapping (visual) of a scoping literature review for an intervention through a community pharmacy to improve services to men, with the workplace playing a strategic role. The interconnecting circles show where the knowledge is; the detached circles show where there are no cross-overs or linkages – this is where the gaps are. This is an example of a scoping

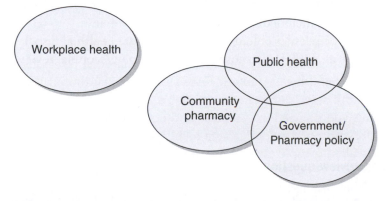

Figure 7.2 Literature scoping map for a project on men's health in community pharmacy

study. Alternatively, it could be labelled as a mapping study. A mapping study helps you assess the size of the work, the terminology used, and the methodological, epistemological and ontological basis of the field. In this example, there was no literature linking workplace health and community pharmacy. By doing this, you will also assimilate knowledge of the range of theoretical approaches.

The plan or protocol

Next, you have to draw up a plan or protocol of the proposed research to establish the theoretical, empirical and conceptual background to your review. You specify the research with a clear aim and objectives, state the research question or questions, and clarify the purpose of the review. The plan helps to establish a degree of objectivity because it is an explicit statement and description of the steps that are to be taken. To complement it, there will be a documented audit of your progress.

To recap, then. Before you can make an explicit plan you have to be aware of the type of information available, the quantity and the quality. This should have been identified during your scoping/mapping review and culminate in the development of your systematic review question. In a limited period of time you will be unlikely to address a complex question that requires the detailed evaluation of thousands of published articles. Conversely, where the topic is relatively new there will be minimal published information available and your review will be easier to complete and relatively short.

Formulating the review question

The review question is critical to the systematic review. The question addressed by the systematic review needs to be defined very precisely because you will have to make a dichotomous (yes or no) decision as to whether each potentially relevant paper will be included or rejected from your review.

Example 7.1 is a policy review problem concerning mental health and social exclusion by Curran et al. (2007). It shows how a mapping/scoping review question was set out.

Example 7.1

A mapping/scoping review question

What empirical evidence is available on the relationship between mental health problems and social exclusion?

Sub-questions

What is the nature of this evidence? Is it qualitative or quantitative?
Which mental health and social exclusion topics are well researched and which are not?
Which countries are the studies set in?
What research designs are used to generate the evidence? (Curran et al., 2007: 293)

More concise guidance on how to frame the question is taken from the Magenta Book (2005). There are four components to designing a systematic policy review question, and these are outlined in Example 7.2.

Example 7.2

Components of a policy review question

1 Give a clear specification of the intervention, factors or processes in question.
2 Give a clear specification of the population or subgroups in question.
3 Give a clear specification of the outcomes that are of interest to the user.
4 Give a clear specification of the contexts in which the questions are set.

By applying these four criteria, we can draw up a systematic review research question about a policy intervention:

What is the effect of a personal adviser service (1. intervention) in terms of retaining (3. outcome [a]) and advancing (3. outcome [b]) lone parents (2. population) in the UK workforce (4. context)?

And an example about implementation:

What are the barriers (1. factors/processes [a]) and facilitating factors (1.factors/processes [b]) to getting lone parents (2. population) to participate (3. outcome [a]) and advance (3. outcome [b]) in the UK workforce (4. context). (Magenta Book, 2005)

Documenting your progress

Throughout the process you have to document your decisions so that the process is transparent to the reader and can therefore be replicated by other researchers. The information you need is usually:

- the title of the database
- date searches conducted
- years covered
- search terms (keywords)
- language restrictions
- number of hits.

Documenting as you go along is crucial because you will obtain a different set of results with every electronic search. You may want to refresh your ideas with a review of the contents of Chapter 2 on library search. The first table you compile will describe the search process. A summary narrative illustration is shown in Example 7.3, which is a systematic review of barriers to recycling in the UK. The documentation can be provided for the reader either in summative narrative form in the report (as in Example 7.3), or in a technical table (Table 7.3).

Example 7.3

The search report from a systematic review 'What are the barriers to recycling' (Jesson and Stone, 2008)

The search began in October 2007 and continued until the final GoogleScholar search in May 2008. A cut-off date of 2001 was deliberately chosen to reflect changes in knowledge about recycling. A systematic search was undertaken of the computerised databases Metalib®, ABI/INFORMS EBSCO, and SWETSWISE. The individual journal databases searched were: Sage, Wiley Interscience online, Oxford, Taylor and Francis Informaworld. Links within these databases to similar journal pages were followed up, as were references at the end of each relevant paper. Once it was noted that one journal was registering frequently, every issue of *Resources, Conservation and Recycling* was scanned for the years 2001–2008 (vols 32–52), which covered our stated timeframe.

The initial electronic search identified 522 papers which contained the words 'barriers to recycling UK'. Each title and abstract was screened using the inclusion/exclusion criteria. Then paper copies were obtained and read more closely for information about barriers to recycling. The final number of papers which met the inclusion criteria was 14. They all had something interesting to say about current barriers to recycling.

The final second GoogleScholar search in May listed 7,090 items using the word string 'barriers to recycling household waste in the UK'. From the first 120 scanned, five new sources, including two conference papers, were identified.

Table 7.3 Search report table (Jesson and Stone, 2008)

GoogleScholar	7,090
e-library electronic databases	522
Potential in scope and interesting	27
In scope after reading	14
Data on current barriers	8

Tip

Documenting your literature search as you go along is good practice and essential in systematic review.

Locating studies and sources of information

Keeping to your plan and research question you can now undertake a comprehensive search for *all* potentially relevant articles or studies through electronic databases. Technical guidance and instructions on searching electronic databases is to be found in Chapter 2. If you are getting too many hits, refine the keywords, synonyms or related terms and do the search again. This stage may be an iterative procedure until you have covered all keyword options.

You will have decided at the planning stage whether the study is to be based solely on electronic sources, as some would advise, or whether you will have to include other material. The range and types of material potentially available were discussed in Chapter 2, but are shown in Figure 7.3.

Academic peer-reviewed articles are said to be the best source of data for systematic review, but an electronic database search can only pick up on the

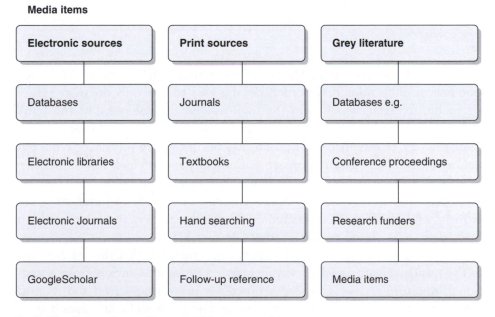

Media items

Electronic sources	Print sources	Grey literature
Databases	Journals	Databases e.g.
Electronic libraries	Textbooks	Conference proceedings
Electronic Journals	Hand searching	Research funders
GoogleScholar	Follow-up reference	Media items

Figure 7.3   Systematic searching: potential resources table

title, subject heading and abstract of the article, as the authors have written it. The authors may not have given sufficient information for the abstract to be picked up and some abstracts give a misleading picture of the contents of the article. Depending on your review question, you may want to widen your search outside the narrow confines of the electronic search to include other methods of searching, such as manual examination of printed journals, and look at other forms of information, such as conference proceedings or commissioned research reports. Check with your supervisor whether this option will be acceptable. There are specific databases in many fields where non-peer-reviewed material is collated, such as www.wastenet.defra.gov.uk, which, in response to the needs of the research community, is beginning to centralise relevant and up-to-date information about waste and resources research.

The search will only be as good as the indexing of the databases you use. But what appears in indexed databases can be just the tip of an iceberg. A Cochrane review of 22 specialist, indexed, UK healthcare journals found that 35% of trials identified by a hand search were not indexed by Medline.

Tip

Following up references and hand searching individual journal contents pages can link you up with supplements, news items, and sometimes letters to the editor, which may have additional information about other research.

The additional steps suggested in the above tip can help you to avoid selection bias or publication bias. Sometimes it is easy to take only the more readily accessible material, which is in the major indexed databases, but this could defeat the aim of scientific rigour that is associated with systematic review methodology. Remember, publication bias occurs where journals have a tendency to promote a given approach and reject papers which have a negative stance or produce inconclusive findings. Therefore, it can be the case that one view predominates in the literature. A public discussion of publication bias arose when leaked emails from climate change researchers at the University of East Anglia was placed on the internet (Pearce, 2010).

So, to summarise the search process so far, remember that the search is one of the standard features which distinguishes a systematic review from a traditional literature review. The search process is more rule-driven and rigorous than in a traditional basic literature review. There has to be an explicit statement of the criteria that are being applied, an attempt, if possible, to cover *all* published material and to state whether any evidence in non-academic forms (such as those in columns 2 and 3 of Figure 7.3) will be used.

Selecting studies: inclusion and exclusion criteria

You only want the articles that help you to answer your research question so the inclusion and exclusion criteria you will apply must be explicit. And you have to set these criteria at the outset, which is why you need a working knowledge of the topic. This is illustrated in Example 7.4. The first stage of your decision-making process is to read the title, the abstract and maybe the introduction and conclusion of the article. You will occasionally find that articles which appear relevant (because of words picked up by the search engine in the title or abstract) are in fact misleading. The second stage is to screen the papers in their entirety, scanning for the key information that you will need for your data extraction (Phase 4 in Table 7.2). This is where the quality criteria are applied and you sort out which papers to include and which to exclude. Assessment involves a degree of subjectivity in the judgements made (Phase 3 in Table 7.2). That is why many systematic review guidelines stress the importance of more than two people independently evaluating each study.

Example: 7.4

The inclusion and exclusion criteria from a systematic review 'What are the barriers to recycling' (Jesson and Stone, 2008)

Keywords
The strings and combinations of keywords included:
'household waste recycling'
'barriers/constraints and recycling'
'marketing and recycling'
'recycling and attitudes/motivation/behaviour and kerbside'

Inclusion and exclusion criteria

Inclusion: English language, UK, domestic waste, household and on street/kerbside studies, empirical evidence of barriers. The time scale was 2001–2008. Grey literature, such as reports and non-academic research, which were identified from reference lists, and GoogleScholar, were considered where available.

Exclusion: outside UK, Civic Amenity (CA) and bring sites only, other aspects of the waste hierarchy – re-use and reduce, measuring participation and set-out rates, volumes of waste, and papers published pre-2001.

You have to document the decisions you make, noting any articles that have been rejected or that failed to meet your criteria and stating why. You may find you will revisit these observations later. Some writers provide a flow chart showing the numbers involved in this process. There is an example in Chapter 8, Example 8.1. The documentation tables are to show the transparency of every decision so that readers can see what you have done.

Appraisal – assessing the quality of research

The next stage in systematic review is the appraisal of the material that you have selected. But how can you do that if you are a novice researcher? If your experience is predominantly in medical, quantitative studies, how can you assess social science or management research based on qualitative studies, or policy-based research? In this section we discuss some of the ready-made tools freely available from internet websites that have been designed by the systematic review centres mentioned earlier.

A key dimension of the appraisal is to examine the methodology of primary studies. There is often a 'quality' threshold applied before a study is included in the review. A 'hierarchy of research study designs' is the model which is used in bio-medical research, but it also sets the standards in other fields of applied research.

This hierarchy is contestable in management and social science fields. The quality of what is accepted as evidence varies by discipline. Medical science has adopted the normal scientific approach, where double-blinded controlled trails are widely accepted as the most rigorous method for testing interventions. Thus random controlled methodology and double-blind, cross-over randomised control trials (RCTs) are known as the gold standard, while qualitative interviews and narrative studies have least credibility and are ranked as anecdotal. The direction of the arrow in Figure 7.4 shows that the higher in the table the method, the better the design quality.

But when we try to apply this judgement across other academic and policy fields of research, such as organisational and business studies, or multidisciplinary social science studies, the limitations of the standard hierarchy of evidence model becomes obvious.

Task

Where in the hierarchy measure do the publications in your area of interest lie? What does it tell you about the nature of research methodology typical in the field?

The gold standard blind randomised controlled trial is rarely used outside clinical research. Trying to impose the randomised controlled method across

Systematic review and meta-analysis

Randomised controlled trials (RCT)

Cohort studies

Case control studies

Cross-sectional surveys

Case reports

Expert opinion

Anecdotal

Figure 7.4 The hierarchy of research study design

organisational or business research is of dubious practical merit and ethical acceptability, and is rarely attempted.

You will spot what constitutes evidence in your field of inquiry as you scan the articles in the search stage. In the waste context, the Department for Environment, Food and Rural Affairs (DEFRA) recognised the limitations of too narrow an evidence base and widened the scope for their *Waste and Resources Evidence Strategy* to include 'more than hard data, facts, trends, survey information but also … judgements and opinions, informal and tacit knowledge and analytical reasoning that sets the data research in context' (DEFRA, 2007).

You have to be pragmatic about using the quality standards. In the 'barriers to recycling' study used as an example in this chapter, it soon became clear that nearly all the studies retrieved were based on a survey method. Thus the quality assessment had to be made on the basis of the details given by the authors of each article about the survey design.

Task

Look at Example 7.6, Tables 7.1 and 2. This is the standard way of presenting summary results of a systematic review. Columns 4 and 5 give methodology details. Now, follow up the original papers yourselves and you will find there is insufficient methodological detail to assess differences in quality for your review.

Note that if the quality criteria are applied too stringently, then you may not have much to review. Ogilvie et al. (2005) reported in their systematic review of public health and health promotion interventions that filtering out studies for exclusion without examining them in any detail would have deprived the reviewers of useful insights and evidence.

Example 7.6

Summary tables (Tables 1 and 2) showing key evidence from a systematic review 'What are the barriers to recycling?' (Jesson and Stone, 2008)

Table 1 Articles included in the systematic review on current barriers to recycling domestic waste

Reference	Aim of research	Focus and location	Method	Non-recyclers Numbers, reasons given
Perrin, D. & Barton, J. (2001) *Resources, Conservation and Recycling,* 33: 61–74	To assess issues associated with transforming household attitudes and opinions into material recovery.	Comparison of two different kerbside schemes. Leeds Bradford	Comparative case study. Door-to-door delivery pre-intervention and follow-up postal self-completion survey. Total sample n = 763	Leeds n = 79 Bradford n = 14 **Barriers listed**
Tucker, P. & Spiers, D. (2003) *Journal of Environmental Planning and Management,* 46(2): 289–307	Attitudes and behaviour change in household waste management.	Home composting. Scotland	Longitudinal case study. Postal survey and deliver/collect. Two samples: those taking up a bin, those not taking a bin. Total sample n = 412/755 No response rate given	Non-composters not counted. Barriers based on the literature and this study. **Barriers listed**
McDonald, S. & Oates, C. (2003) *Resources, Conservation and Recycling,* 39: 369–385	To understand the non-recycler better.	Reasons for not opting-in to take a kerbside container. Sheffield	Case study. Postal survey non-participants only. Total sample n = 714/1690 Response rate 43%	Content analysis. Coded barriers into 12 categories. **Barriers listed**
Thomas, C., Yoxon, M., Slater, R. & Leaman, J. ISWA World Congress (2003)	To explore reasons why people recycle linked to a public communications and education campaign.	Kerbside provision. London Boroughs Western Riverside	Longitudinal case study. Part one. MORI face-to-face interview survey of n = 2023 and 13 focus groups.	Segments: medium, high, low and non-recyclers. **Barriers listed**
Williams, I.D. & Kelly, J. (2003) *Resources, Conservation and Recycling,* 38: 139–159	To identify reasons for non-participation in green waste collection.	Green waste opt-in or opt-out of a taking a container. Wyre, Lancashire	Case study. Two stages and two samples. Opt-in participants response rate 72.5% Opt-out response rate 49%	Non-participators n = 611 **Barriers listed**

Table 1 (Continued)

Reference	Aim of research	Focus and location	Method	Non-recyclers Numbers, reasons given
Robinson, G.M. & Read, A.D. (2005) *Resources, Conservation and Recycling*, 45: 70–83	To assess kerbside and bring site behaviour and promotional activity.	Measuring changes over time, 2000–2004. Royal Borough of Kensington and Chelsea	Longitudinal case study. One in four household sample, face-to-face interviews. Samples: 2000: n = 8,066 2004: n = 3,367	Percentage non-recyclers drops from 51% to 27% **Barriers listed**
Smallbone, T. (2005) *Business Strategy and the Environment*, 14: 110–122	To measure consumer views on household waste and test assumptions underlying policy approach.	Recycling behaviour. England, Scotland, Wales	Includes a NOP national telephone survey. Sample n = 1000	Non-recyclers 21% **Barriers listed**

Table 2 Articles excluded from the systematic review and reasons

Reference	Aim of research	Focus and location	Method	Reason for exclusion
Davis, G. Phillips, P.S., Read, A.D. & Lida, Y. (2006) *Resources, Conservation and Recycling*, 46: 115–127	Understanding recycling participation using the Theory of Planned Behaviour.	Testing theory to create effective targeting material. West Oxfordshire	Survey hand delivered to 334 houses. Sampling: ACORN A, DEF, part of B. Response rate 22%	Excluded non-recyclers from analysis (n = 2). **Not about barriers**
Shaw, P.J., Lyas, J.K., Maynard, S.J. & van Vugt, M. (2007) *Journal of Environmental Management*, 83: 34–43	To assess kerbside schemes using a mathematical model based on SOR and PR.	To prioritise campaigning. London Borough of Havering	Street observation and Survey sample n = 4,085.	Literature review only
Oates, C.J. & McDonald, S. (2006) *Sociology*, 40(3): 417–433	To investigate recycling as domestic labour.	Gendered division of labour. Sheffield	Postal self-completion survey. Sample n = 469/1,532 Response rate 31%	**Not about barriers**

(Continued)

Table 2 (Continued)

Reference	Aim of research	Focus and location	Method	Reason for exclusion
Karousakis, K. & Birol, E. (2008) *Journal of Environmental Management* (internet version)	To examine the determinants of household recycling behaviour, measure willingness to pay.	London Boroughs of Kensington and Chelsea, Richmond upon Thames and Westminster	On street interviews Sample n = 188.	**Not about barriers**
Barr, S. (2007) *Environment and Behaviour*, 39(4): 435–473	To develop and test a conceptual framework.	Exeter	Self-completion survey. Contact and collect method. Sample n = 673/981 Response rate 69% Literature review and theory.	**Not about barriers**

There are a range of checklists that you can draw on to appraise the quality of non-clinical research. For example, we have provided the COREQ 32 checklist (Tong et al., 2007) in Appendix 2 (and see below). This checklist was written as formal reporting guidelines to help authors and journal reviewers improve the quality of work that is submitted to and published in medical journals, but the ideas are transferable to other disciplines.

Some researchers have found that the hierarchy of evidence model limits their choice and have devised a personalised quality hierarchy relevant to the topic or field. For example, in a meta-analysis of a study on stigma and mental health, quality was assessed along four dimensions: theory, publication bias, research design and sources of heterogeneity (Mak et al., 2007). Unlike the hierarchy of evidence which measures research design quality, Table 7.4 shows how to measure the quality of publication. Publication bias assesses external validity, or the extent to which the results can be generalised to the population.

Assessing quantitative studies

The previous section described the appraisal of study design using the hierarchy of evidence model and a customised four-dimensional quality appraisal model. The usual way to assess the quality of an individual study is to examine key features of the article or report. The following list is just some of the key dimensions that you could use as a starting point:

Table 7.4 Variables in assessing study quality, examining external validity

Dimension of quality assessment	Components and operational definitions	Measure
Type of review process	Has the paper undergone peer review?	• Peer reviewed • Not peer reviewed (grey)
Publication type	Where is the article published? This list may vary according to the protocol	• Academic journal • Professional journal • Book or book chapter • Doctoral dissertation
Publication date	When was the article published?	• Before 2000 • 2000 and later
Journal impact factor, for prestige, where 5 is highest	What is the current impact factor of the journal in which the paper is published?	• 0–1.0 • 1.1–2.0 • 2.1–3.0 • 3.1–4.0 • 4.1–5.0

Source: Adapted from Mak et al. (2007)

The introduction

Are the aim and objectives of the study clear?
Why was the study undertaken? (Known as the rationale)
Why now, in this context?
Is there a link to theory?

Method

What is the research design?
Is there detail about the sampling frame, how and why the sample was selected?

Data

What types of data are there?
How and where, and by whom was the data produced?
How trustworthy, reliable and valid is the data?

Analysis

How was the data analysed?
How rigorous and trustworthy is the analysis?

Results
Are the results a true representation of the data?
Do the results relate back to the research question?
Do the authors discuss the methodological limitations of their study?

Assessing qualitative studies

When it comes to assessing or appraising qualitative research there are several published guidelines to help you. Tong et al. (2007) undertook a systematic review of the many guidelines that have evolved to assess the quality of qualitative studies, covering in-depth interviews and focus group techniques, to produce The Consolidated Criteria for Reporting Qualitative Studies (COREQ). This is a 32-item checklist based on 76 items from 22 checklists which you might find useful (see Appendix 2). The comprehensive 32-item list can be adapted to suit your research field.

Assessing management or organisational studies

Systematic reviews have traditionally been applied in fields of research where positivist and quantitative approaches are dominant. Consequently, far less has been written about how to do a systematic review in some other fields of research, such as management. As mentioned earlier, Tranfield et al. (2003) explain that management research is a comparatively young field of inquiry, which is far less well developed than medical science. Nevertheless, there are a number of original reviews being undertaken by groups of researchers in several fields of inquiry that are being published in the *International Journal of Management Reviews*. There is not, as yet, a specific or appropriate published checklist to assess management research, so for your own review read the existing criteria list and then draw up your own criteria for assessing your specific field of study.

Data extraction

Now you have retrieved your articles, there will be two piles of papers in front of you (if you have printed them off), or two bibliography lists if you prefer that approach. One pile IN and one pile OUT. You have documented the process so far, and accounted and explained why the articles are in each pile. The next stage is to extract the relevant data from the articles in the IN pile.

Every researcher has his or her own favourite way of highlighting key aspects from articles; some insights were given in Chapters 5 and 6. One way to start, probably the old-fashioned way, is to highlight sections of the paper with highlighter pens, and then enter the relevant information on to your data extraction form. This might be another dynamic phase where you revise the format of what you want to record. You may want to revisit the scoping and mapping phase, or revise your inclusion and exclusion criteria.

Example 7.5

The data extraction form from a systematic review 'What are the barriers to recycling' (Jesson and Stone, 2008)

The data extraction form has to reflect the question and planned assessment. It is another visual record of the decisions you have made. It will include the following details:

(a) Author and publication details (bibliographic details)
(b) Paradigm (academic discipline)
(c) Aim and focus of the paper
(d) Method details (sample selection, size, method design, response rate, location of the study)
(e) Theory or models
(f) Data about barriers to recycling (either as a literature review/summary or numbers of non-recyclers or a list of new reasons or barriers)
(g) Segmentation
(h) Other relevant or useful information

You will soon have several completed data extraction forms. You can then move on to the next phase and undertake your analysis and synthesis.

Synthesis, drawing conclusions, what the review shows

The analysis and synthesis is probably the most intellectually taxing phase of the systematic review process. Hart (1998: 110) defined synthesis as 'the act of making connections between the parts. It is not simply a matter of re-assembling them back into the original order but of finding a new order.' In the data extraction stage you unpacked each article. In the synthesis stage you have to put them all together again, but this time telling a new story or making new connections. That is your contribution to knowledge, or filling the knowledge gap.

There is no single agreed way of synthesising the evidence; it will depend on the type of review and subject matter. The aim is to collate and present the extracted data from primary studies so that the characteristics and results of the study are summarised in a meaningful way.

There are two components to synthesis: (1) the story, and (2) the table (the evidence). Descriptive or non-quantified studies involve narrative text and *tabulation* to present the study characteristics and results – in essence a short summary of findings. You will not need to tabulate all the data. Select the important points which help to answer your question, and structure them to highlight the similarities and differences between the included studies.

Tabulation allows the reader to scan down the columns and see where the similarities and differences are. The second component, where it may be possible in some studies to quantify synthesis by using statistics, is described in Chapter 8.

Evolving formats of systematic review

So far this chapter has described the process used to produce a systematic review. This process is 'protocol'-driven and follows a systematic methodology. We have also observed that this methodology was introduced to deal with biomedical and healthcare research studies. Business, organisational and social science researchers have been slower to adapt it for their requirements. Some researchers argue that systematic review is not appropriate for policy and management decisions, and you may have come to that conclusion for yourself by this point. For those who are still curious, carry on reading.

The controversial big question for reviewers has been 'Is it feasible to combine the findings of research studies that use different methods? The following section briefly introduces some of the more recent innovations and adaptations to the systematic methodology. These are more advanced, complex and specialised review methodologies, which may be useful for doctoral students.

Systematic reviews of qualitative and quantitative research

To date, there is no single agreed framework for synthesising both qualitative and quantitative data. A challenging contribution by Mays et al. (2005) explores this issue in one of several articles in the special edition on synthesising evidence in the *Journal of Health Services Research and Policy*, supplement to issue 3 (2005). Mays et al. (2005) proposed four basic approaches to synthesising both qualitative and quantitative types of data to inform policy making in the field of health. The four approaches are:

- Narrative, which includes traditional literature reviews, thematic analysis, narrative synthesis, realist synthesis and meta-narrative mapping.
- Qualitative, which converts all available evidence into a qualitative form using techniques such as meta-ethnography and qualitative cross-case analysis.

- Quantitative, which converts all evidence into a quantitative form using techniques such as quantitative case survey or content analysis.
- Bayesian meta-analysis and decision analysis.

In 2005, when the journal supplement was published, non-biomedical systematic reviews were in their early stages of development. Two examples of more recently published articles are presented in Example 7.7 to illustrate the methodological approaches.

Example 7.7

A meta-narrative mapping analysis (Collins and Hayes, 2010)

Met-analysis mapping is defined as the process of plotting how a particular research tradition has unfolded over time. It is an approach which combines the analytical dimensions of traditional narrative research with the comprehensiveness and rigour pursued in systematic literature reviews (Collins and Hages, 2010: 10). This is said to be a useful technique in the synthesis of vast and complex evidence bases to inform policy processes.

The aim of this review was to monitor thematic trends in the health inequalities knowledge base over time and to map local government intervention on local health inequalities. The reviewers searched for four bodies of knowledge: health promotion, Healthy Cities, population health and urban health, covering a 20 year timeframe 1986–2006, using only abstracts (therefore text as written, qualitative data). The timeframe represents the evolution of health determinants research. 1004 abstracts were reviewed. The lens applied was Canadian. Three electronic databases were searched. The result is a bibliographic report, which describes the detail of each article, showing the quantitative changes over the timeframe and the qualitative change in emphasis of topics and prescriptions for government intervention.

There are some points to note about this review and to show how you can use articles to generate research questions. First, it is based entirely on abstracts. Hopefully you will now be aware of some of the limitations associated with abstracts, so apply your critical lens to the paper. Second, note that the search ended in 2006 and the article was published in 2010, reflecting the time to carry out the search, review and synthesis, and then add on more time to write up the article and finally get it published. So, third, it would be perfectly possible to take this review as a starting point for a new review and see what has been published on the topic since that 2006 cut-off date. Or it could be possible to widen the databases search, maybe applying a European lens or possibly including grey literature.

Further specialist advice on thematic analysis is freely available online at the ESRC National Centre for Research Methods.

Grey literature in systematic reviews

One of the obstacles that policy researchers have identified with the systematic review methodology is that adopting a method used successfully in the clinical biomedical sciences is not automatically applicable in other fields of knowledge. A key issue is that in social sciences and policy research much of the useful knowledge is contained in non-academic, non-peer-reviewed journals, in so-called grey literature (Curran et al., 2007; Collins and Hayes, 2010).

The reason this is a problem is that grey literature is at the bottom of the academically acceptable resources table (Table 7.3) and does not register at all in the hierarchy of research study design (Table 7.4). Another limitation is in actually identifying this type of resource because academic electronic databases do not pick them up. This is where a working knowledge of the topic is essential, or maybe your information specialist in the library can help. If you do not access grey literature you are excluding that valuable information from service users, charitable organisations, think tanks, and so on. This is essentially an argument about what counts as knowledge in your field. The final obstacle is how to analyse, synthesise and incorporate the material you are allowed to use.

Umbrella reviews

Systematic reviews have been completed on many subjects and we are approaching the stage when it is possible to analyse the systematic reviews themselves as a body of knowledge. These are known as umbrella reviews. An umbrella review is a way of identifying and appraising and synthesising existing systematic review evidence. As such they are able to present the overarching findings of existing systematic reviews (see Example 7.8).

Example 7.8

Tackling the wider social determinants of health and health inequalities: evidence from systematic reviews (Bambra et al., 2009)

A systematic review methodology was used to locate and evaluate published and unpublished [therefore grey literature] systematic reviews of interventions around the 'wider social determinants of health' (Bambra et al., 2009). The authors set the context of an increasing policy emphasis on tackling the 'wider social determinants of health' through the implementation of appropriate interventions. So the aim of the review (or to put it another way, the research question) was to identify what is already known and to highlight areas for further development. The review identified 30 relevant systematic reviews and concluded that the effects of interventions on health inequalities were unclear.

So, what might the limitations be of a review of reviews? Without reading each review, and then reading each article or report within each review, the reader is relying on the skills, knowledge and expertise of Bambra and colleagues to be reliable interpreters of qualitative, quantitative and grey literature. So is the review still as reliable as a protocol-driven methodology would suggest it should be?

─────────────────────── Summary ───────────────────────

This chapter has given guidance on how to undertake a systematic literature review using a defined protocol, where the data is fairly homogeneous. We concluded by considering whether it is feasible to undertake a systematic review with data that are not homogeneous or with grey material that may not be acceptable to your academic institution. The answer is left open because this is an ongoing debate. Finally, some observations about objectivity and bias are necessary. It would be irresponsible to pretend that this methodology is entirely free from bias. As researchers, we make judgements at every stage of the review process. Occasionally, some bias may be unconsciously made as a result of the ideological lens through which we read each article. Then we need to make a decision on its quality and relevance.

Remember, systematic review is a question-driven methodology. If you do not have a specific question, you should probably be doing a traditional review. If you are reviewing research with quantitative data, then meta-analysis could be the way to synthesise the data, and that is the subject of Chapter 8.

8

META-ANALYSIS

Key Points

- Meta-analysis is a *statistical* technique to combine data on the size of a measured effect from different published sources, to produce an estimate of the overall effect size
- A good working knowledge of statistical methods is required to complete a meta-analysis
- Meta-analysis requires the computing of a summary statistic for each study, and the calculation of an average of those summary statistics
- The researcher must be able to choose an appropriate meta-analysis method for their data, and to interpret its findings
- The robustness of the conclusions of a meta-analysis should be tested by performing a sensitivity analysis

Be aware

- Your meta-analysis is very dependent upon the quality of the systematic review that produced the data to be combined
- Bias in meta-analyses can occur, for example due to selection bias or publication bias
- Do not attempt to combine the data from dissimilar studies

Overview

This chapter can be considered on its own by students wishing to become familiar with the purpose, procedures and terminology of the technique of meta-analysis. We believe that a book on literature review would be incomplete without this chapter. The main focus here is on clinical studies, but the guidance is transferable and relevant to all disciplines where published quantitative data has been produced to address the same hypothesis. Tranfield et al. (2003: 217) observed that in management research there are few studies which address the same research question or measure the same phenomenon in the same way. To date, researchers in these fields have been more concerned with understanding organisations and management processes. Therefore, it is unlikely that meta-analysis will be an appropriate approach. Nevertheless, we have identified a few studies which have used meta-analysis (see Table 8.1 below).

However, for students wishing to conduct a meta-analysis, an understanding of the systematic review method covered in Chapter 7 is essential. Meta-analysis is a statistical method of combining quantitative data from several different studies to produce new data. As such, the means by which the component studies for the meta-analysis have been identified becomes vital to the objectivity and quality of the results obtained. The old adage 'garbage in garbage out' applies as much to the research methods of systematic review and meta-analysis as it does to other methods of data analysis. This chapter uses a question-and-answer format to describe meta-analysis.

In Chapter 7 you have become familiar with the purpose of a systematic review of the literature and its key stages, as described in Table 7.2. It is worth reiterating here that a systematic review has a clearly stated purpose (often phrased as a question), clearly defined methods for searching for information, for quality appraisal, and explicitly stated criteria for inclusion and exclusion from the study. The outcome of a systematic review could be a table summarising relevant details from the studies included in the review, with a narrative interpretation of the overall results of the systematic review. This is sometimes referred to as a 'meta-review' and may be a useful addition to previous knowledge. However, it does require skill in interpretation of data to avoid accusation of bias. The technique of meta-analysis has been developed to improve the objectivity of quantitative results and their interpretation.

It may be the case that the type or quality of the data obtained in your systematic review means that no further analysis is possible. If so, then revisit Chapter 7 for advice on appropriate qualitative synthesis of results. If you are unsure, or think that your data may be suitable for further statistical analysis, read on.

What is meta-analysis?

Meta-analysis is a statistical technique which has been developed to combine quantitative results obtained from independent studies that have been published. You can easily find a definition of 'meta-analysis' using an internet search, but two definitions I have found useful are given here.

Greenhalgh (2006: 122) describes meta-analysis as a specialised type of systematic review which is used for quantitative studies; it is a 'statistical synthesis of the numerical results of several trials which have addressed the same question'. This quotation encompasses several key features of a 'good' meta-analysis that we will return to later, and was written with clinical science in mind. In comparison, Petticrew and Roberts (2006: 19) defined meta-analysis for a social science audience as 'a review that uses a specific statistical technique for synthesising the results of several studies into a single quantitative estimate (the summary size effect)'. Both these definitions emphasise summarising and statistics.

But why is a meta-analysis useful or indeed needed? Petticrew and Roberts (among others) assert that traditional (narrative) reviews are more likely to reach uncertain conclusions because of a lack of systematic search for *all* material and a dependence on the individual skills, views and agenda of the researcher. In addition, the motivation in the clinical sciences can be the same (that is, to find an objective measure of the truth), but can also be about making best use of the vast resources needed when conducting clinical trials of new drugs or therapies.

In the field of medical science, where evidence-based medicine is a defining principle, the technique of systematic review of clinical trials of a therapeutic intervention followed by meta-analysis of the data obtained has led to more certainty as to the benefit (or otherwise) of the intervention than any of the individual trial results were able to provide. Thus in a case where several trials of the efficacy of a drug in a particular patient group (for example) had provided only weak evidence of effectiveness, meta-analysis of data already in the public domain may provide robust evidence of a treatment effect. One reason for this is the greater statistical power achieved when the results of many smaller studies are combined.

It has taken many years for the validity and value of meta-analysis to be appreciated. Indeed, their use is still uncommon in many areas of inquiry. Since the 1980s they have been popular in the fields of behavioural, social and medical science, where they are now considered to be at the top of the hierarchy of evidence for effectiveness of medical or other healthcare interventions (see Figure 7.4).

Convincing evidence of the value of the meta-analysis technique can be found in the work of Fergusson et al. (2005), who performed a cumulative meta-analysis on 64 randomised control trials investigating the effect of the drug Aprotinin on the outcome of cardiac surgery. The first trial included in the meta-analysis was performed in 1987, and Fergusson et al. showed that had someone undertaken a meta-analysis of the first twelve trials between that date and 1992, they would have shown a statistically significant effect of the treatment. So, thereafter there should have been no more need for further trials designed to answer the same question. However, a meta-analysis was not done at that time and the authors list a further 52 trials which were performed between 1992 and 2002, all of which could be deemed unnecessary.

Can I use meta-analysis to summarise the results of my systematic review?

The simplest form of meta-analysis uses what is called a 'fixed effect model' for statistical analysis. This type of analysis assumes there is one main effect which will be investigated (not many different variables), and that the data from all the studies to be combined in your meta-analysis is homogeneous. Homogeneous data means that, in statistical terms, the data is from the same population. In real terms it means that the results of the individual trials are compatible with one another. Results of studies *may* not be homogeneous if:

- the study designs are different
- if the sample of patients/subjects varies between trials or studies
- if different outcome measures are used
- or if the quality or size of the studies is different.

There are statistical methods that try to identify the heterogeneity of data (see below), but as they are of low statistical power it is often more important that the researcher studies the data in tabular or graphical form in addition to using statistical tests (see Figures 8.1 and 8.2 below). Make sure you plot the results of all the individual trials on a graph using a common scale. You should look for any evidence of heterogeneity (which would invalidate or alter the type of meta-analysis done) between the individual trials data.

How can you tell if the results of your literature search have produced data that can be combined in a meta-analysis? Tabulation of results, as illustrated in Tables 1 and 2 in Example 7.6, is a vital stage of the systematic review methodology because it allows the researcher (and the reader of the review) to compare the methodological details of each study, and to compare the outcomes reported in each study or trial. You cannot perform a meta-analysis if the data cannot be obtained, or is very limited. It may be that the outcome measure in studies or trials can be manipulated such that comparable data is obtained (for example, by calculation of an odds ratio, see Table 8.1 and Figure 8.4), or comparable data can be extracted from the information published. Again, a good working knowledge of the area is needed to ensure that any manipulations undertaken are meaningful and appropriate.

Table 8.1 Examples of effect size data used for meta-analyses in three research areas

Examples from medical research: health interventions

Odds ratio: number of patients who respond to a treatment divided by the number of patients who do not respond.
Relative risk: number of patients who respond to a treatment divided by the total number of patients.
Mean change in clinical measurement, for example change in blood pressure following treatment or control, or before and after a treatment.
Prevalence rates of a disease.

Examples from psychology

In a meta-analysis of roles of person and situation factors on workplace safety (Christian et al., 2009):

Safety climate: many variables including safety systems, supervisor support, job risk and work pressure.
Leadership.
Personality characteristics: conscientiousness, neuroticism, extraversion, locus of control, propensity for risk-taking.
Attitudes: safety, job.

In a meta-analysis investigating the effect of error management training (Keith and Frese, 2008):

Type of outcome measured: within training performance or post-training performance.
Type of transfer: analogical or adaptive.
Clarity of feedback task: high or low.
Comparison used: procedure-based training or exploratory training.

Examples of economic evaluations

Usually cost–benefit calculations. In cost–benefit analysis of a medical intervention (Pang et al., 1999), the benefit is often calculated as clinical effectiveness, using the outcome criteria for medical research listed above (odds ratio, relative risk, etc).

In an ongoing meta-analysis of the economic impact of road improvements schemes (Highways Agency, 2009), factors in the analysis were split into:

Non-monetised benefits or costs, such as effect on heritage or impact on water resources.
Factors on which a monetary value could be placed, which included effect of schemes on journey times, on accidents and on vehicle operating costs.

I have been using the term 'outcome measure' to mean the data from each individual publication in a review that is to be combined in a meta-analysis. That is because my background is biomedical research, and meta-analysis is commonly used to combine clinical trial data which measure the outcome of a particular treatment. However, the general concept that you need to understand is that meta-analysis combines data which measure an 'effect size' to provide an estimate of the combined effect size. An 'effect size' is something that encodes *any* research findings on a numerical scale, thus making it suitable for statistical manipulation. Table 8.1 shows some 'effect sizes' that have been used in published meta-analysis from different research specialisations. If your area of interest is not here, look at a range of publications relevant to the topic and identify which data presented might be an 'effect size' in terms of the technique of meta-analysis.

When you have collected and evaluated the publications to be included in your review and meta-analysis, you should start by considering three things:

1   Are the effect sizes reported in each publication the same?
2   Does the variability reported in the results (effect sizes) suggest they are from a homogeneous population?
3   Is the summary of the data produced by your meta-analysis meaningful?

We will take these one by one here.

Do the individual publications in your review report similar effect sizes?

The effect size that you use for your review may be determined by the availability of data in your area of specialisation, and by any guidance or protocols that exist for research in your field of interest. An example of an area of research where the design of trials and the outcome measures reported in clinical trials are controlled is in the investigation of the effect of new treatments for cancer. Testing new treatments for any life-threatening condition is ethically difficult, and because of this the World Health Organisation (WHO) developed a standardised clinical trial reporting format as long ago as 1979. This defined not only reporting structure, but also some outcome measures (such as objective response rate). One of my project students performed a systematic review summarising the evidence for effectiveness of a new treatment for HER2 positive meta-static breast cancer. Because of the WHO guidance in this field, and other regulatory requirements, the trial designs (including clear definitions of disease state and other inclusion criteria) and primary outcome measures used (for example, time to progression and response rate) in publications are often very similar, which made meta-analysis of the results easier and possible. This is because the data produced effect sizes that were consistent between the individual studies.

However, in other research fields where there is less consensus on suitable and appropriate outcome measures, or where researchers' ability to control their research design is not as great, we find that the published data is highly varied. This was true in the field of pharmacy-based public health interventions, where another student attempted a systematic review of the literature to examine whether there was evidence for a public health benefit of such interventions. A systematic search in 2008 (limited to publications relating to interventions in England and Wales, and only those in a community pharmacy setting) identified a small number of publications. Over a third of the publications were excluded as their results focused on the views and attitudes of the pharmacist involved, rather than on any public health outcome. Ten publications were included in the final review, and these reported using five different research designs. Each studied a different intervention and each used very different outcome measures of health benefit. These outcome measures ranged from self-reported smoking cessation with nicotine validation, through self-reported adherence and blood pressure measurements, rates of unprotected sex, to full economic evaluation of the intervention. There were no consistent effect sizes to combine. A statistical meta-analysis of this type of data was obviously inappropriate. The details of the inclusion and exclusion criteria for this project, plus a summary of the studies identified is shown in Example 8.1 (compare the presentation style in this figure with Examples 7.3 and 7.4).

Example 8.1

Inclusion and exclusion criteria developed for a student project of community pharmacy-based public health interventions, carried out in 2008/09

Question component	Inclusion criteria	Exclusion criteria
The population	Populations in England receiving pharmaceutical interventions	Any population outside England
The interventions	Any intervention carried out by a community pharmacist	No intervention carried out by a community pharmacist, or an intervention carried out by a hospital pharmacist
The setting	Community pharmacy premises	Hospital, home-based, clinic-based or GP practice-based
The time period	Studies carried out (and published) between 1998 and 2008	Studies carried out prior to 1998
The study	All experimental and observational studies	Any editorial comments, systematic reviews, case reports or case studies without comparators
Publication and search	English language only, searched for using online resources at Aston University	

Example 8.1   Continued

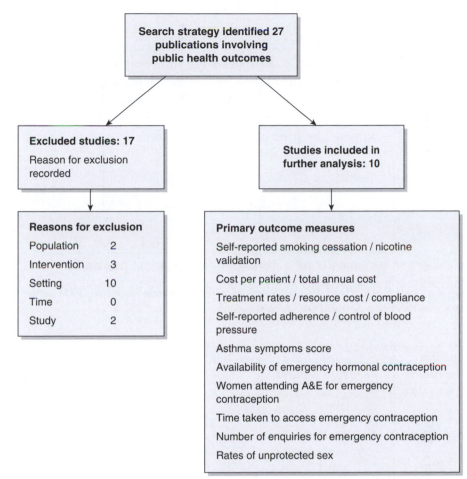

Are the results of individual trials in your review from a homogeneous population?

A quick, but potentially inaccurate, way of assessing this is to view the graphical representation of the data from each independent study. Are the mean results (the effect size) comparable and is there evidence of non-homogeneity? This is similar in principle to looking at a graph of mean and standard error measured in two groups: if the error bars do not cross, we might suspect the groups are different. Have a look at Figures 8.1 and 8.2. The results for the four imaginary trials in Figure 8.1 have very similar means and their error bars are all similar in size and cross over each other. I would say that there is no visual evidence that these trials are heterogeneous. Once again the hypothetical data presented is from my area of interest, but the principle can be applied to any numerical data.

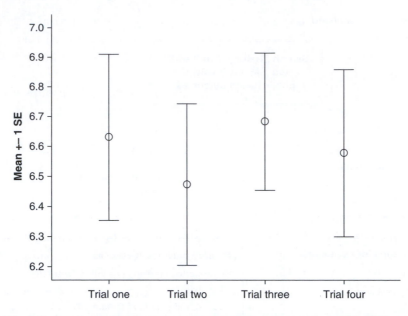

Figure 8.1 Data from four trials appears homogeneous: similar means and variability (SEM plotted). Data is imaginary and drawn using SPSS for Windows Release 12.0.1

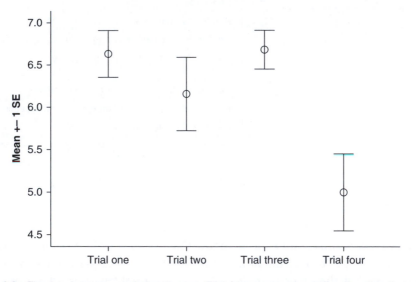

Figure 8.2 The data here appears heterogeneous: Trial 4 has a mean lower than the other three, and the variability of the data from the trials differs. The data is imaginary and is drawn using SPSS for Windows Release 12.0.1

The data reported in Figure 8.2, however, is different. Three of the imaginary studies look very similar, although the error bars are of different size (suggesting different variability in results, but the significance of this can be dependent upon how the variability is expressed). However, trial four has a very different mean, and error bars (standard error of the mean) that do not cross those of the first three studies. For Figure 8.2, I would say there *is* visual evidence that the results are *not* homogeneous.

How can we tell if my 'guess' as to the homogeneity of the groups was correct? I would test it statistically. The data plotted in Figures 8.1 and 8.2 were mean and standard error of the mean (SE), obviously coming from continuous data given the descriptive statistics used. The outcome measures of many trials are often *not* continuous or normally distributed. Therefore, parametric statistical tests (such as Students t-test) to tell the difference between groups should not normally be used. To confirm (or refute) suspicions of heterogeneity you would be better to use a statistical test which does not rely on assumptions of normality, such as the Chi-square test ($\chi 2$). This test assumes that all the variability seen in the data is due to chance (the null hypothesis of the test), and calculates whether there is evidence that this null hypothesis can be rejected. So, the larger the value of $\chi 2$ the less likely that the data is homogeneous. As a general rule, results are deemed 'statistically different' if the p value for the calculated $\chi 2$ statistic is less than or equal to 0.05 (most computer-based statistical tests will calculate the test statistic and its corresponding p value for you). However, as noted before, the $\chi 2$ test does not have great statistical power. That is, there has to be quite a large difference in the data before the test will say that there *is* a significant difference between the groups. The effect of this statistical nicety is that we stand a chance of coming to an incorrect conclusion that the data *is* homogeneous, and therefore *can* be combined in a meta-analysis when in fact the groups *are* different but the test has not been sensitive enough to pick up the difference. Therefore, we should always confirm the robustness of conclusions from our meta-analysis with sensitivity analysis if possible (see 'Is my meta-analysis free from bias?' below).

Are my results meaningful?

You may find that some effect sizes are common to all your independent studies, but that there are other measurements which are reported in some studies and not others. Which outcome measures (effect sizes) should you use in your meta-analysis? There are two things to consider: is the data suitable (back to homogeneity), and which combined data is *meaningful?* This is where *you* have to know enough about your topic area to decide which effect sizes can and should be combined to give meaningful results in the context of the purpose of the research. To use an obviously fictitious example: ten trials of a new washing powder all measured the time taken to dissolve 100g of the product at 30°C. In addition, each trial reported a different measure of cleaning ability. It would be tempting for the meta-analyst to choose the dissolution time as a suitable measurement to combine and summarise because it is common to all the trials, but does it actually help address the research question, which is 'which powder will get my washing cleanest?'

Undertaking your meta-analysis

Once you have summarised the results of each of the studies you are including in your review, and selected or generated an appropriate outcome measure (effect size) for meta-analysis, then you can use statistical methods to combine the data. A meta-analysis calculates a standardised mean effect size from the individual data. As this is not a detailed statistical text we will refer you now to the more authoritative information sources given in Appendix 4. Most people today use statistical packages, such as RevMan, to store and analyse their data. This is the one used for preparing reviews for the Cochrane Collaboration Review Manager (RevMan, 2008). These programs often offer a number of different methods of meta-analysis. Which one do you use? There are a couple of statistical concepts which are worth addressing here so that you are less likely to choose the wrong method of meta-analysis. If you have found that it is most likely that the results of the individual trials in your review are homogeneous, then you can use a method based on a fixed effect model, which is where we can assume that changes in a clinical measure are caused by one factor. You can then combine the data to produce a *pooled effect estimate* and a measure of the variability of that estimate (usually 95% confidence intervals).

If, however, a statistical test has shown that your data are from a hetero-geneous population, then you must use a method based on a random effects model (a multi-level or multivariate analysis). In this method there is an assumption that the variability between studies is normally distrib-uted. Random effects models produce an estimate of the *mean treatment effect*, with its associated confidence interval *and* a measurement of the *variance* between the studies. This can be used to help researchers identify causes of variability other than the main effect size (or variable) effect. To take another example from my field of biomedical research which will illustrate this point: heterogeneity in the effects of a new drug was found between three randomised control trials which included data from men and women. A second analysis was performed looking at the new drug on men only. In this analysis the difference between the trials disappeared. This shows that the first analysis has identified a gender difference in the effect of the drug, and it was this gender difference which explained the heterogeneity of data found when the drug effects on both the sexes were combined.

In summary, if your data *is* heterogeneous, you can't just ignore it and perform a simple meta-analysis. It is, however, an opportunity to find a reason for the different effects of the treatment in different studies.

Do all studies I have identified contribute in the same way to my meta-analysis?

An important part of any systematic review (with or without meta-analysis) is to critically evaluate the quality of the individual trials you have identified. This forms part of the inclusion/exclusion criteria, but also forms a central part to the weighting that each study or trial is given in your meta-analysis. For example, if your review has identified ten randomised control trials, all using the same drug, at the same dose, with the effect size measurement on the same number of people, then it is sensible to make a simple estimate of the 'average' effect (the pooled effect). However, if you have identified trials which employed different research methods (see hierarchy of design, Figure 7.4) or employed very different numbers of participants, then it would not be valid to give the same weight to the outcome of each trial. You may indeed choose to exclude trials with low 'quality' scores from your analysis, and the impact of doing this can be checked by performing a sensitivity analysis (see below).

Factors identified in the field of medical research that affect the quality of the data from a clinical investigation include randomisation to treatment, blinding of patient and practitioners to treatment, size of trial group, outcomes measured, internal sensitivity of measurements made, methods of analysis and presentation used. If meta-analyses are already common in your area of research, you may find that other researchers have already developed and tested scales for assessing the quality of individual publications. If, however, you are among the first to use meta-analysis in your field, you may find you have to develop (and test) quality assessment criteria yourself. This may be the case with management studies, an issue raised in Chapter 7 in relation to systematic review.

Displaying the results of a meta-analysis

The output from a meta-analysis is usually a pooled estimate of the mean effect size across the studies included in the review, plus a measure of the variability of that estimate (confidence limits). A common way of presenting this data is to show the effect size measurements (plus their confidence limits) from the individual trials plus the pooled estimate on the same diagram. This allows you to visually check the variability between the effect sizes reported in individual studies and that the pooled estimate is a reasonable 'average' of those results. In Figure 8.3 Lewis and Clarke (2001) describe the history of forest plots and their use in meta-analyses. The results of a meta-analysis are shown in the form of a forest plot (sometimes known as a blobbogram).

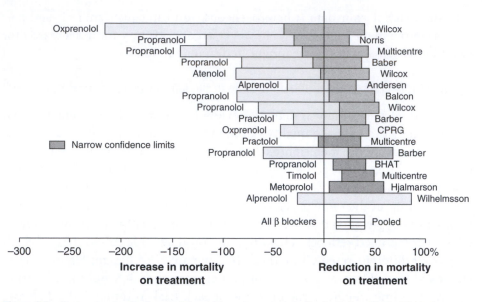

Figure 8.3 First example of a forest plot used in meta-analysis to illustrate the effect of β blocker drugs on mortality (Lewis and Clarke, 2001: 1479)

Figures 8.3 and 8.4 are the data from the same meta-analysis shown in two different ways. The units on the *x*-axis of the diagram will vary depending on the effect size being investigated, and therefore care in interpreting the results is needed. In Figure 8.3 the effect size is the percentage change in mortality following treatment, with the vertical line representing no difference in the number of deaths in the control or the treatment group. The same data is shown in Figure 8.4, where an odds ratio has been used as the effect size measurement.

Therefore in Figure 8.4, a mean pooled estimate lying to the left of this line implies that the treatment has had an effect (an odds ration <1) whereas odds ratios greater than one (to the right of the line) suggest that the drug actually increases mortality. The dotted line is the pooled estimate of mean odds ratio. The effect measured was mortality; therefore treatments that reduce mortality (whose effect is to the left of the central line) are to be favoured. This illustrates how the results of meta-analyses have to be interpreted in the context of both how they are displayed and what effects they represent. Here we are hoping for a reduction in the outcome effect measured, whereas in other investigations an increase in the effect might be the desired outcome.

Is your meta-analysis free from bias?

We have already discussed how important the systematic review stage of meta-analysis is in terms of being focused, comprehensive, clear in inclusion and quality assessment methods. These all help to reduce bias in the resulting

Study	No (%) of deaths β blocker	No (%) of deaths Control	Patients Logrank observed − expected	β blocker deaths Variance of observed − expected	Ratio of crude death rated (99% CI) β blocker: control
Wilcox (oxprenolol)	14/157 (8.9)	10/158 (8.9)	2.0	5.6	
Norris (propranolol)	21/226 (9.3)	24/228 (9.3)	−1.4	10.2	
Multicentre (propranolol)	15/100 (15.3)	12/95 (12.6)	1.2	5.8	
Baber (propranolol)	28/355 (7.9)	27/365 (7.4)	0.9	12.7	
Andersen (alpranolol)	61/238 (25.6)	64/242 (26.4)	−1.0	23.2	
Balcon (propranolol)	14/56 (25.0)	15/58 (25.9)	−0.2	5.5	
Barber (practolol)	47/221 (21.3)	53/228 (23.2)	−2.2	19.5	
Wilcox (propranolol)	36/259 (13.9)	19/129 (14.7)	−0.7	10.5	
CPRG (oxprenolol)	9/177 (5.1)	5/136 (3.6)	1.1	3.3	
Multicentre (practolol)	102/1533 (6.7)	127/1520 (8.4)	−13.0	53.0	
Barber (propranolol)	10/52 (19.2)	12/47 (25.5)	−1.6	4.3	
BHAT (propranolol)	138/1916 (7.2)	188/1921 (9.8)	−24.8	74.6	
Multicentre (timolol)	98/945 (10.4)	152/939 (16.2)	−27.4	54.2	
Hjalmarson (metoprolol)	40/698 (5.7)	62/697 (8.9)	−11.0	23.7	
Wilhelmsson (alpranolol)	7/114 (6.1)	14/116 (12.1)	−3.4	4.8	
Total*	640/7047 (9.1)	784/6879 (11.4)	−81.6	310.7	

Axis: 0   0.5   1.0   1.5   2.0
β blocker better | β blocker worse
Treatment effect $P < 0.0001$

Reduction 23.1% (SE5.0) P<0.001
Heterogeneity between 15 trials: $\chi^2 = 13.9$; df = 14; P > 0.1

* 95% confidence interval as shown for the odds ratio

Figure 8.4 Data in Figure 8.4 replotted using ratio of death rate in control versus treatment (odds ratio, OR) as effect size. OR = 1 means no treatment effect; OR<1 implies the drug treatment reduces death rate; OR>1 means that death rate increases with treatment (Lewis and Clarke, 2001: 1480)

meta-analysis of data. However, your review will probably be limited to *published* information, therefore publication bias may be a factor in the conclusions you draw from your data. Studies showing the beneficial effect of a new treatment (or, indeed, any positive finding in your area of interest) are more likely to be published than those showing no effect. You can use a funnel plot to examine whether your results have been influenced by publication bias (or any other form of bias) (Eggar et al., 1997). A funnel plot maps the size of the effect measured (x-axis) against the precision of the measurement in each study (y-axis: inverse of variance, usually related to sample size). The theoretical basis for the funnel plot is that high-quality, large studies are more likely to provide good estimates of a true effect, and therefore there should be little variability between such studies (greater precision). Similarly, there should be more variability in the effect sizes reported for smaller or lower quality studies.

If there is no publication bias, you would expect a funnel shaped, symmetrical plot, where the more precise studies (higher on the y-axis) tend to be grouped together, and the less precise studies (lower down the y-axis, usually smaller, but could be low quality) have a wide range of outcomes. This is illustrated by Sutton et al. (2000) and in Figure 8.5 (the top block), which shows the type of data you would expect if publication bias was not a significant factor.

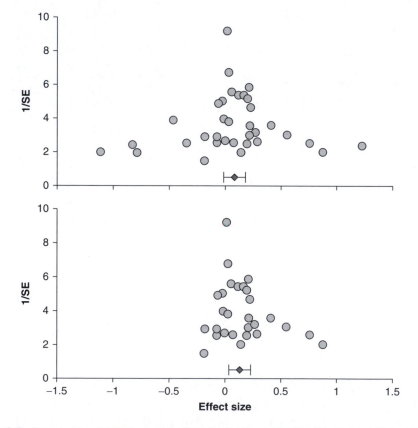

Figure 8.5 Funnel plot suggesting no publication bias (top) or publication bias (bottom) (Sutton et al., 2000: 1575)

If publication bias in your included studies *is* a factor, then the plot will not look symmetrical. Figure 8.5 (the lower block) is a good example of a funnel plot showing publication bias. Here there seem to be no smaller trials which report negative effects.

It may be possible to accommodate for publication bias in a meta-analysis by adding in data to replace that which is apparently 'missing' due to publication bias (see Figure 8.6), and therefore to produce a second pooled estimate of effect. However, you would need to be very confident that the distribution of data was indeed due to publication bias before such a technique could be used. The filled circles in Figure 8.6 denote the imputed missing studies. The bottom diamonds show summary effect estimates before (open) and after (filled) publication bias adjustment (Hopkins and Small, 2006).

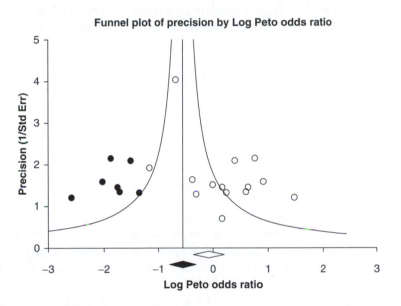

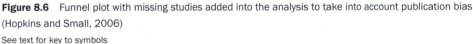

Figure 8.6 Funnel plot with missing studies added into the analysis to take into account publication bias (Hopkins and Small, 2006)

See text for key to symbols

Performing a sensitivity analysis

Now we will briefly discuss how you can tell whether the pooled effect size estimate calculated by your meta-analysis is robust, or whether you have included some bias during any stage of your data collection and evaluation. Sensitivity analysis allows you to assess what happens to the results of your meta-analysis if you change a certain parameter – that is, if you change the inclusion criteria of your review or some other important assumption or variable in your data. This allows you to test whether you have indeed identified the correct mathematical model to use for your analysis, whether you have coded your data correctly, or whether you have in fact introduced bias into your findings.

Sensitivity analyses compare the results of two or more meta-analyses of the same dataset, calculated using different assumptions. You look to see whether the result of each sequential meta-analysis is the same as the first, or if changing one parameter changes the outcome of the analysis. One example would be performing a sensitivity analysis to determine whether there is a difference in the conclusions of your meta-analysis if you included unpublished results in your analysis. First, you would calculate your mean effect size using all the data you have collected from your systematic search. Next, you would repeat the analysis but this time exclude data from all unpublished material. Was there a difference in the mean effect size calculated from the two analyses? Similarly, you could perform a sensitivity analysis to determine the effect of date of publication on the outcome of your meta-analysis.

The results of a sensitivity analysis will allow you to determine whether the findings of your study are robust or whether they are affected by the methods used to obtain them. The Cochrane Collaboration expects a sensitivity analysis of all their published reviews.

Summary

This chapter provides you with an introduction to meta-analysis which does not attempt to explain the mathematical details of the method, but highlights the technique's relationship to and dependence on the systematic review methodology. As with any area of research, you may be limited by the availability of the data or by the nature or quality of the data available. Consideration of these points is key to undertaking useful systematic reviews with meta-analysis of data, and coming to valid conclusions. Indeed, you may find that some published meta-analyses are themselves biased for reasons of the methodology employed. To help you further with these concepts, the publications listed in Appendix 4 may be of use. They come from my own area of medical research, but cover general principles which may be of use to students of many disciplines.

9

REFERENCING AND PLAGIARISM

Key points

- Check which referencing system you are required to use
- Learn the recommended style (for example, the exact order of elements in the reference, fonts, punctuation) and apply it consistently throughout your references. Sometimes software for managing references can help with this
- Accurate referencing is good practice because it helps readers who may want to follow up your work

Be aware

- Institutions are routinely using plagiarism detection software to cross-check the content of work against previously published work
- To avoid unintentional plagiarism, make clear notes about your sources – how you have located them, recording full citation details and your own responses
- Remember that all material (whether printed or electronic) is protected by copyright

---

Introduction

You have now reached the end phase of 'doing a literature review'. Sources of information have been identified through the library search. You have read and reflected, summarised and analysed until you are confident that you know enough about the topic. Along the way you have made notes that have helped you to write up the review. The final activity now is to compile an accurate reference list.

We have emphasised throughout this book the importance of documenting every source you use as you go along, so that compiling the final list should not pose many problems. There are several different systems of referencing. If you are writing a paper for university or college, check with your department which system you need to use and learn how to use that system accurately, taking into account the order of the elements of the reference, the font styles and the punctuation. Many institutions will provide style guidelines so check with your academic department or your librarian whether guidelines, online tutorials or reference management software such as EndNote™ or Reference Manager™ are available. In addition, some word-processing tools include referencing features such as the option to insert citations and references from templates for different systems.

If you are using referencing software, such as EndNote™ or Reference Manager™, then the process is straightforward and the software does most of the work for you. You may be very confident in your knowledge of referencing systems, in which case you can skim read this chapter. The advice offered here is based on frequently asked questions of library staff from students.

Why is referencing important?

Citing references is an important part of academic research because:

- references acknowledge the contribution of the work of others and their place within the area of research
- they provide evidence to the reader of the range and breadth of sources you have used.

According to Pears and Shields (2008: 11), they 'establish the credibility and authority of your ideas and arguments'. In addition, your references are an important source of research in their own right, so it is vital they are accurate and complete. Moreover, correct referencing and citation will ensure that you avoid any danger of unintentional plagiarism.

What do you need to reference?

You should always include in your references any materials you have directly referred to in your text. When you have consulted sources, but not directly referred to them in your text, you can include these sources in your bibliography (if there is one).

Note that the distinction between reputable, published sources and unpublished sources, known as grey literature, has become less clear with online publishing. Accurate references are therefore particularly important to help the reader identify and locate all sources to check for quality and authority.

How many references should I provide?

Students often ask 'How many references should I provide?' The answer is not straightforward because how many references to include depends on the expectations of the assessor, the level and depth of the work and the subject area. Some areas of research will have an enormous amount of published material to draw on, whereas others may have very little. The important factor is to complete your research correctly and to document this by illustrating your methods (see Chapter 2, in particular Table 2.3).

When and how to reference

Neville (2010: 19) writes about six scenarios of when to reference (see Table 9.1). Table 9.2 then shows how these scenarios can be referenced using the two most common systems: the Harvard and the Numeric systems.

Table 9.1 When to reference: six scenarios (Neville, 2010: 19)

1 To inform the reader of the source of tables, statistics, diagrams, photographs and other illustrations included in your assignment
2 When describing or discussing a theory, model, practice or example associated with a particular writer; or using their work to illustrate examples in your text (this links specifically to the next two items)
3 To give weight or credibility to an argument supported by you in your assignment
4 When giving emphasis to a particular theory, model or practice that has found a measure of agreement and support amongst commentators
5 To inform the reader of the sources of direct quotations or definitions in your assignment
6 When paraphrasing another person's work, which is outside the realm of common knowledge, and that you feel is particularly significant, or likely to be a subject of debate.

Referencing systems

You can learn your recommended referencing system by following examples from a published journal article or book chapter, or alternatively by seeking detailed guidance in the texts listed below. The main systems are:

- Name/date in the text – known as the Harvard system.
- Numeric and running notes in the text – also known as the Vancouver system.
- Name/date – American Psychological Association (APA). For the APA system consult: American Psychological Association (2005), *Concise Rules of APA Style*.
- Name/page number – Modern Language Association (MLA) of America. For the MLA system refer to: Gibaldi (2003), *The MLA Handbook for Writers*.
- Legal documents have a separate referencing system. In the UK, the most widely used system is the Oxford Standard for Citation of Legal Authorities (OSCOLA) developed by the Faculty of Law, Oxford University (see: www.denning.law.ox. ac.uk/published/oscola.shtml).

Table 9.2 The Harvard and numeric referencing systems

	Examples of referencing using the name/date (Harvard) system	Examples of referencing using the numeric system
In-text citation – summary	There are six scenarios where evidence must be referenced in assignments (Neville, 2010).	There are six scenarios where evidence must be referenced in assignments (1).
In-text citation – paraphrasing	According to Neville (2010), there are several different scenarios where evidence must be referenced in assignments. These include providing the reader with sources of data or quotations included in your assignment, describing or giving weight or emphasis to an argument or theory and paraphrasing someone else's work.	According to Neville (1) there are several different scenarios where evidence must be referenced in assignments. These include situations to provide the reader with sources of data or quotations included in your assignment, describing or giving weight or emphasis to an argument or theory and paraphrasing someone else's work.
In-text citation – quotations	There are several reasons why writers must include references. As Neville has stated, one of the situations where you will need to reference evidence is: 'When paraphrasing other person's work, which is outside the realm of common knowledge, and that you feel is particularly significant or likely to be a subject of debate' (Neville, 2010: 19). Pears and Shields (2008: 11) state that references can also 'Demonstrate that you have spent time in locating, reading and analysing material and formed your own views and opinions.'	There are several reasons why writers must include references. As Neville has stated, one of the situations where you will need to reference evidence is: 'When paraphrasing another person's work, which is outside the realm of common knowledge, and that you feel is particularly significant or likely to be a subject of debate' (1). Pears and Shields state that references can also: 'Demonstrate that you have spent time in locating, reading and analysing material and formed your own views and opinions' (2).
References	NEVILLE, C. (2010). *The complete guide to referencing and avoiding plagiarism*, 2nd edn. Maidenhead: Open University Press. PEARS, R. & G. SHIELDS. (2008). *Cite them right: the essential referencing guide*. Newcastle upon Tyne: Pear Tree Books.	1. NEVILLE, C. *The complete guide to referencing and avoiding plagiarism*, 2nd edn. Maidenhead: Open University Press, 2010. 2. PEARS, R. & G. SHIELDS. *Cite them right: the essential referencing guide*. Newcastle upon Tyne: Pear Tree Books, 2008.

For detailed examples of how to reference all types of information (printed and electronic), using any system, consult Neville (2010). In Table 9.3 column one lists a range of documents that you may need to reference and columns 2 and 3 show how to reference in each of the two basic styles.

Table 9.3 A range of document types showing the Harvard and numeric styles of referencing

	Examples of references using the name/ date (Harvard) system	Examples of References Using the Numeric System
Printed book	NEVILLE, C. (2010). *The complete guide to referencing and avoiding plagiarism.* Open University Press study skills. Maidenhead: Open University Press.	NEVILLE, C. *The complete guide to referencing and avoiding plagiarism.* Open University Press study skills. Maidenhead: Open University Press, 2010.
Electronic book	NEVILLE, C. (2007). *The complete guide to referencing and avoiding plagiarism,* 2nd edn. [Online]. Open University Press study skills. Maidenhead: Open University Press. Available from: http://lib.myilibrary.com [Accessed 1 Dec. 2009].	NEVILLE, C. *The complete guide to referencing and avoiding plagiarism.* [Online]. Open University Press study skills. Maidenhead: Open University Press, 2007. Available from: http://lib.myilibrary.com [Accessed 1 Dec. 2009].
Printed book with three or more authors	SAUNDERS, M. et al. (2009). *Research methods for business students.* Harlow: Prentice Hall.	SAUNDERS, M. et al. *Research methods for business students.* Harlow: Prentice Hall, 2009.
Chapter within edited printed book	LAZONICK, W. (2006). The innovative firm. In J. FAGERBERG (Ed.), *The Oxford handbook of innovation.* New York: Oxford University Press, pp. 29–55.	LAZONICK, W. The innovative firm. In J. FAGERBERG (Ed.), *The Oxford handbook of innovation.* New York: Oxford University Press, 2006, pp. 29–55.
Chapter within edited electronic book	LAZONICK, W. (2006). The innovative firm. In J. FAGERBERG (Ed.), *The Oxford handbook of innovation.* [Online, 2009]. New York: Oxford University Press, pp. 29–55. Available from: http://www.oxfordhandbooks.com/ [Accessed 1 Dec. 2009].	LAZONICK, W. The innovative firm. In J. FAGERBERG (Ed.), *The Oxford handbook of innovation.* [Online, 2009]. New York: Oxford University Press, 2006, pp. 29–55. Available from: http://www.oxfordhandbooks.com/ [Accessed 1 Dec. 2009].
Printed journal article	ELLERY, K. (2008). Undergraduate plagiarism: a pedagogical perspective. *Assessment and evaluation in higher education.* Vol. 33, no. 5, pp. 507–516 (10).	ELLERY, K. Undergraduate plagiarism: a pedagogical perspective. *Assessment and evaluation in higher education.* 2008, Vol. 33, no. 5, pp. 507-516 (10).
Electronic journal article	GRAY, K. et al. (2008). Web 2.0 authorship: issues of referencing and citation for academic integrity. *Internet and higher education.* [Online]. Vol. 11, no. 2, pp. 112–118. Available at: http://www.sciencedirect.com [Accessed 1 Dec. 2009].	GRAY, K. et al. Web 2.0 authorship: issues of referencing and citation for academic integrity. *Internet and higher education.* [Online]. 2008, Vol. 11, no. 2, pp. 112–118. Available at: http://www.sciencedirect.com [Accessed 1 Dec. 2009].
Printed newspaper	ROBSHAW, B. (2009). Many students simply don't know how to reference. *Independent, Education,* 15 Oct. 2009, p.4.	ROBSHAW, B. Many students simply don't know how to reference. *Independent, Education,* 15 Oct. 2009, p.4.

(Continued)

Table 9.3 (Continued)

	Examples of references using the name/ date (Harvard) system	Examples of References Using the Numeric System
Electronic newspaper	ROBSHAW, B. (2009). Many students simply don't know how to reference. *Independent, Education.* [Online]. 15 Oct. 2009. Available from: http://www. lexisnexis.com [Accessed 1 Dec. 2009].	ROBSHAW, B. Many students simply don't know how to reference. *Independent, Education.* [Online]. 15 Oct. 2009. Available from: http://www.lexisnexis.com [Accessed 1 Dec. 2009].
Website	NEVILLE, C. (Ed.) (2007). *Learn Higher: avoiding plagiarism.* Bradford: Learn Higher at Bradford University. Available at: http://www.learnhigher.ac.uk/site/ index.php [Accessed 1 Dec. 2009].	NEVILLE, C. (Ed.) *Learn Higher: avoiding plagiarism.* Bradford: Learn Higher at Bradford University, 2007. Available at: http://www. learnhigher.ac.uk/site/index.php [Accessed 1 Dec. 2009].
Thesis	JESSON, J.K. (1988). *Ethnic minority builders: a comparative study of Britain and the United States of America on affirmative action in the building industry.* Unpublished PhD thesis. Aston: University of Aston.	JESSON, J.K. *Ethnic minority builders: a comparative study of Britain and the United States of America on affirmative action in the building industry.* Unpublished PhD thesis. Aston: University of Aston, 1988.
Electronic report	OXFORD STANDARD FOR CITATION OF LEGAL AUTHORITIES. (2006). Available at: http://denning.law.ox.ac. uk/published/oscola.shtml [Accessed 1 Dec. 2009].	OXFORD STANDARD FOR CITATION OF LEGAL AUTHORITIES. 2006. Available at: http://denning. law.ox.ac.uk/published/oscola.shtml [Accessed 1 Dec. 2009].
Online tutorial	MARTINDALE, C. et al. (2006). [Online Tutorial Version 1]. *Plagiarism learning and teaching online: PLATO.* Derby: Innovation 4 Learning at the University of Derby. Available online at: http:// www.i4learn.co.uk/education [Accessed 1 Dec. 2009].	MARTINDALE, C. et al. [Online Tutorial Version 1]. *Plagiarism learning and teaching online: PLATO.* Derby: Innovation 4 Learning at the University of Derby. 2006. Available online at: http://www. i4learn.co.uk/education [Accessed 1 Dec. 2009].

Where to find the citation information you need

It is important to obtain the citation information directly from the source that you are using.

- Information for your reference list can generally be found on the title page inside the book.
- For journal articles, the information is often found on the first page of the article.
- For online sources or databases there may be a 'credits' or 'about' page, which will provide citation information for the online source as a whole.
- Some online resources and databases provide facilities to save citations, so look out for 'citation', 'cite' or 'export' links. This can be a very useful feature which can save you time if the referencing system provided matches the system you

need to use. If this is not the case, then you can still export the data, as it will provide all the information you require, but you will need to re-order the elements and restyle that information into the format your institution or department adopts.

When checking different referencing systems for particular items such as books or newspapers, the WorldCat online catalogue (www.worldcat.org/) allows you to search for items and then cite/export the reference information from their catalogue, selecting the reference system that you need to use. Selections can be made from APA, Harvard and the MLA systems. Search for items on the catalogue and select the Cite/Export feature.

The illustration in Table 9.4 gives an example of different citation systems and styles for a book (Neville, 2007) that was obtained through the facility to cite from the WorldCat catalogue. In this example the elements of information are the same but their order changes as well as the name format, font styles and punctuation. Once you know which style you will be using, it is important to apply that style consistently to all of your references.

Figure 9.1 shows the citation information in the Harvard system provided through the WorldCat catalogue for Denzin and Lincoln (2005), *The Sage Handbook of Qualitative Research*.

Table 9.4 Citation styles for *The Complete Guide to Referencing and Avoiding Plagiarism* (Neville, 2007)

APA

Neville, C. (2007). The complete guide to referencing and avoiding plagiarism. Open UP study skills. Maidenhead: Open University Press.

Chicago (Author-Date)

Neville, Colin. 2007. The complete guide to referencing and avoiding plagiarism. Open UP study skills. Maidenhead: Open University Press.

Harvard

NEVILLE, C. (2007). The complete guide to referencing and avoiding plagiarism. Open UP study skills. Maidenhead: Open University Press.

MLA

Neville, Colin. The Complete Guide to Referencing and Avoiding Plagiarism. Open UP study skills. Maidenhead: Open University Press, 2007.

Turabian

Neville, Colin. The Complete Guide to Referencing and Avoiding Plagiarism. Open UP study skills. Maidenhead: Open University Press, 2007.

Plagiarism

Referencing is an integral part of academic research. Thorough research alongside complete referencing will help to give your work credibility and authority

Figure 9.1 WorldCat catalogue showing citation for Denzin and Lincoln (2005)

The screenshot was taken from OCLC's WorldCat database and is used with OCLC's permission. WorldCat® is a registered trademark of Online Computer Library Center, Inc.

while avoiding any perception of plagiarism. The whole concept of academic prestige is built on confidence that the work is genuinely that of the author. However, with the growth of online information and the use of word-processing to write up work, the potential for plagiarism is greater than ever.

You may decide to copy and paste from an online source as a way of making notes to highlight some key points as you do your research. However, it is really important to put quotation marks around that information and to reference it immediately in your own notes so that you avoid unwittingly reusing that material in your own work at a later date. Remember that if you have found material online, then others can also find the same material through an online search. Plagiarism detection software is routinely used within academic institutions to detect plagiarism from online sources. Unintentional plagiarism can be avoided by keeping very clear notes on your research as you go along.

How can I avoid being accused of plagiarism?

Read the following passage from Jesson and Stone (2008). This article was written specifically for use in this book so that we avoid any danger of plagiarism or falling foul of copyright laws.

Jesson, J. and Stone, I. (2008) *What do we currently know about barriers to recycling household waste in the UK? – a literature review*. Research Working Paper RP 0915. Birmingham: Aston Business School. www.abs.aston.ac.uk or www.m-e-l.co.uk. Accessed July 2009.

> Researchers have been writing about recycling since the 1970s but, as many subsequent authors note, results are frequently contradictory and complicated by differences in waste collection schemes. In 1995 Hornik et al. published a synthesis of the determinants of recycling behaviour, drawing on international material mainly from the USA covering the years 1970–82. A similar collation of current knowledge is to be found in Tucker and Spires' (2003) *monographs*, which also incorporates international knowledge. This early material is descriptive and focuses on the why, what and how questions. Several studies continue to argue the case for more research into barriers and how they might be overcome (for example, McDonald and Oates, 2003; Thomas et al., 2004; Robinson and Read, 2005; Martin et al., 2006).

Example Student 1

> Researchers have been writing about recycling since the 1970s but, as many subsequent authors note, results are frequently contradictory and complicated by differences in waste collection schemes. Several studies continue to argue the case for more research into barriers and how they might be overcome.

Comment 1

This review is totally inadequate because there is no mention of the original source (Jesson and Stone, 2008). The student uses the original words and ideas as their own, without acknowledging the authors. The words are quoted directly and the work does not use any of the traditional devices, such as inverted commas (quotation marks), italics or indentation to show that this is the original source. So, this is plagiarism.

Example Student 2

> The recycling literature dates back to the 1970s. A systematic review (Hornik et al., 1995) and a summary by Tucker and Spiers (2003) covers the main articles. We can conclude from these reviews that the results of early research are frequently contradictory and complicated by contextual differences. Moreover, the research is predominantly descriptive.

Comment 2

This review is better because the student has acknowledged the contributions of Hornik et al. (1995) and Tucker and Spiers (2003). But it does not acknowledge that the original critique of the review (*frequently contradictory and complicated by contextual differences; the research is predominantly descriptive*) was made by Jesson and Stone (2008). They are therefore claiming the 'critique' as their own analysis. This is cheating.

Example Student 3

In a summary review of the literature on recycling Jesson and Stone concluded that 'results are frequently contradictory and complicated by differences in waste collection schemes' (2008: 13). However, it could be argued that Jesson and Stone have been overly critical of the early studies. They have failed to report on the positive aspects and useful lessons learnt from earlier studies that have now been incorporated into modern services.

Comment 3

In this third example the student has credited the original words and critical observation of the original authors. So, there is no plagiarism here. The student then goes on to provide a personal critique of the article itself, using his/her own words. This is what we are looking for – an original interpretation of the knowledge.

So remember:

- Acknowledge the <u>words</u> of other writers.
- Acknowledge the <u>ideas</u> of other writers.
- The point is to add to what is already known, so always make clear which are your arguments ('it could/can be argued' is a useful phrase).

Inappropriate referencing or inaccurate citation can cause problems for later researchers. Citation errors can lead to distortions in knowledge, which is misinformation that can lead to bias in future research. It is always best to go back to original papers and check the information that you are citing.

Copyright

Being aware of copyright rights is important because it is one way we respect the intellectual property of others. While you are doing your research remember that all materials are protected by copyright, including those made available on the internet. This means that you will need to reference correctly and obtain permission from the copyright holders before publishing any copyrighted material. As a user of library resources, it is important also to note that licence agreements do not normally allow you to provide access to any subscription-based online materials, including journal articles, to other people. In addition, there are often limitations on how much you can download and how long you can save online resources to your own computer. If in doubt, check the copyright statements and licence agreements of online resources or speak to your academic librarian.

Conclusion

References can frequently become an important research resource in their own right. If your literature review was to be published as a journal article, then your references could be made available to others in a bibliographic database to be used by other researchers to track research in your field of interest. Bibliographic databases, such as Web of Knowledge, contain a huge number of references, which can then be used in different ways to rank publishing by particular authors or journals or to track research over time through citations forwards and backwards in time. References are an incredibly valuable source of data for researchers who want to trace source material and original research as well as ongoing developments. References have a long life-cycle and can become an historical source for research.

--- Summary ---

This chapter provides guidance on why referencing is important, what you need to reference and how to reference. It also highlights some tools which can help with compiling references. Documenting your search is part of the process and software tools can automate the process. Acknowledging others' ideas, avoiding plagiarism and an awareness of copyright issues are all integral to academic research.

APPENDIX **1**: FURTHER READING

Books

Aveyard, H. (2007) *Doing a Literature Review in Health and Social Care*, Maidenhead: Open University Press.

Cottrell, S. (2005) *Critical Reading Skills: Developing Effective Analysis and Argument*, Basingstoke: Macmillan.

Dolowitz, D., Buckler, S. and Sweeney, F. (2008) *Researching Online*, Basingstoke: Palgrave Macmillan.

Fink, A. (2005) *Conducting Research Literature Reviews: From Internet to Paper*, London: Sage.

Greenhalgh, T. (2006) *How to Read a Paper: The Basis of Evidence-based Medicine* (BMJ Books), Oxford: Blackwell.

Hart, C. (1998) *Doing a Literature Review: Releasing the Social Science Imagination*, London: Sage.

Hart, C. (2000) *Doing a Literature Search*, London: Sage.

Kahn, K.S., Kunz, R., Kleijnen, J. and Antes, G. (2003) *Systematic Reviews to Support Evidence-based Medicine*, London: Royal Society Medicine Press.

Mays, N., Pope, C. and Popay, J. (2005) Systematically reviewing qualitative and quantitative evidence to inform management and policy making in the health field, *Journal of Health Services Research and Policy* 10 (Supplement 1): 6–20.

Petticrew, M. and Roberts, H. (2006) *Systematic Reviews in the Social Sciences: A Practical Guide*, Oxford: Blackwell.

Ridley, D. (2008) *The Literature Review: A Step-by-step Guide for Students*, London: Sage.

Torgerson, C. (2003) *Systematic Reviews*, London: Continuum.

Online

Magenta Book for government policy evaluation: www.policyhub.gov.uk

Medicine: www.evidence-based-medicine.co.uk

Social care research: www.scie.org.uk

APPENDIX 2: CRITICAL REVIEW CHECKLIST (LINKED TO CHAPTER 7)

COREQ 32-item checklist (Tong et al., 2007).

Domain 1: Research team and reflexivity

Personal characteristics

1   Interviewer/facilitator. Which author(s) conducted the interview or focus group?
2   Credentials. What were the researcher's credentials? For example, PhD, MD.
3   Occupation. What was their occupation at the time of the study?
4   Gender. Was the researcher male or female?
5   Experience and training. What experience or training did the researcher have?

Relationship with participants

6   Relationship established. Was a relationship established prior to study commencement?
7   Participant knowledge of the interviewer. What did the participants know about the researcher? For example, personal goals or reasons for doing the research?
8   Interviewer characteristics. What characteristics were reported about the interviewer/facilitator? For example, bias, assumptions, reasons and interests in the topic?

Domain 2: Study design

Theoretical framework

9   Methodological orientation and theory. What methodological orientation was stated to underpin the study? For example, grounded theory, discourse analysis, ethnography, phenomenology, content analysis.

Participant selection

10   Sampling. How were participants selected? For example, purposive, convenience, consecutive, snowball.

11 Method of approach. How were participants approached? For example, face-to-face, telephone, mail, email.
12 Sample size. How many participants were in the study?
13 Non-participation. How many people refused to participate or dropped out? Why? What reasons did they give?

Setting

14 Setting of data collection. Where was the data collected? For example, in the home, clinic, workplace.
15 Presence of non-participants. Was anyone present beside the participants and researchers?
16 Description of sample. What are the important characteristics of the sample? For example, demographic data, date.

Data collection

17 Interview guide. Were questions, prompts, guides provided by the author? Was it pilot tested?
18 Repeat interviews. Were repeat interviews carried out? If yes, how many?
19 Audio/visual recording. Did the research use audio or visual recording to collect the data?
20 Field notes. Were field notes made during and/or after the interview or focus groups?
21 Duration. What was the duration of the interview or focus groups?
22 Data saturation. Was data saturation discussed?
23 Transcripts returned. Were transcripts returned to participants for comment and/or correction?

Domain 3: Analysis and findings

24 Number of data coders. How many data coders coded the data?
25 Description of the coding tree. Did authors provide a description of the coding tree?
26 Derivation of themes. Were themes identified in advance or derived from the data?
27 Software. What software, if applicable, was used to manage the data?
28 Participant checking. Did participants provide feedback on the findings?

Reporting

29 Quotations presented. Were participant quotations presented to illustrate themes/findings? Was each quotation identified? For example, with a participant number.
30 Data and findings consistent. Was there consistency between the data presented and the findings?
31 Clarity of major themes. Were major themes clearly presented in the findings?
32 Clarity of minor themes. Is there a description of diverse cases or discussion of minor themes?

APPENDIX **3:** SYSTEMATIC REVIEW – ONLINE RESOURCES (LINKED TO CHAPTER **7**)

Here are some of the useful links to organisations which provide freely downloadable systematic review resources.

Campbell Collaboration for Social Interventions. Campbell Collaboration covers social and behavioural interventions and public policy, criminal justice and social welfare. www.campbellcollaboration.org.uk

CASP. Public Health Resource Unit. This organisation has been developing its work since 1993. It provides an evaluation base for health and social care. The site has seven types of systematic review critical appraisal tools which cover: reviews, randomised control trial (RCT), qualitative research, economic evaluations, cohort studies, case control studies, diagnostic test studies. www.pru.nhs.uk

Centre for Reviews and Dissemination (CRD), University of York, which undertakes reviews in health and social care effectiveness. www.york.ac.uk/inst/crd

The Cochrane Collaboration. Cochrane is the major centre for clinical and biomedical systematic reviews. www.cochrane.org

Cochrane health promotion and public health field. www.ph.cochrane.org and www.vichealth.vic.gov.au/cochrane

EPPI-Centre. Evidence-informed Policy and Practice, National Centre for Research Methods, Social Science Research Unit, London. This centre has been developing its tools since 1993. It collates evidence for policy and practice on: education, health promotion and public health, employment, social care, crime and justice. www.eppi.ioe.ac.uk

ESRC National Centre for Research Methods. Thomas, J. and Harden, A. (2007) *Methods for the Thematic Synthesis of Qualitative Research in Systematic Reviews*, Working paper series 10/07. www.ncrm.ac.uk

Government Social Research Civil Service. Rapid appraisal toolkit for quantitative and qualitative studies. www.gsr.gov.uk/professional_guidance/rea_toolkit

Social Care Institute for Excellence (SCIE). This site has a systematic review manual for the conduct of reviews in social care. www.scie.org.uk

APPENDIX 4: RESOURCES FOR META-ANALYSIS (LINKED TO CHAPTER 8)

The following sources of information may be of use to those wishing to improve their understanding of meta-analysis in the clinical sciences.

Bandolier: Evidence-based medicines publications at www.medicine.ox.ac.uk/bandolier

- What is evidence-based medicine?
- What is meta-analysis?
- Bandolier bias guide
- The importance of size
- On quality and validity

There are many texts discussing both fixed effect models and random effects models, some of which are beyond this amateur statistician! For a useful comparison of the two methods see:

Van Den Noortgate, W. and Onghena, P. (2003) Multilevel meta-analysis: a comparison with traditional meta-analytical procedures *Educational and Psychological Measurement*, 63: 765.

Statistical packages performing meta-analysis can be found from a simple internet search. The examples below are for information, and are not personal recommendations.

- Comprehensive meta-analysis: www.meta-analysis.com/pages/demo.html
- Meta-Stat: www.echo.edres.org:8080/meta/metastat.htm
- Mix: www.mix-for-meta-analysis.info/
- NCSS: www.ncss.com/
- RevMan: www.cc-ims.net/revman

GLOSSARY

Abstract. A summary of an academic paper, which gives an overview.

Analyse. A detailed examination of the parts of something. Think of a scientist in a laboratory looking through a microscope, showing the essence by breaking the object down into component parts, examining each part in detail and showing how the parts fit together.

Argument. Having an opinion and arguing that point of view, presenting the case for and/or against a particular proposition, backed up by evidence.

Article. A paper on a specific topic, published in an academic journal. The good ones are usually refereed for quality by peers.

Bias. Showing a particular disposition or prejudice that colours the way something is interpreted.

Bias, publication. Publication bias is a recognised phenomenon in which positive results have a better chance of being published, are published earlier, and are published in journals with higher impact factors. Thus reviews based only on published data may themselves be biased.

Bias, statistical. In statistics, bias occurs when the calculated (or estimated) value of something is different from its true value. This can be caused by many things, including biased sampling methods, choice of statistical analysis, external factors causing systematic bias or publication bias.

Bibliographic database. Provides a search interface for articles, keywords and references, covering many publications, a wide time and geographic span.

Bibliographic details. Details that allow a reader to locate the source (name, date, title, place of publication and publisher).

Bibliographic list. A compilation list of sources that cover a given topic, usually in alphabetical order.

Bibliographic referencing tools. Software such as Endnote™, Reference Manager™, for managing references.

Blobogram. Another term used for a forest plot (see below).

Boolean operators. AND, OR, NOT.

Citation. The name and date of a resource used or referred to in a text, which is presented in full in a reference list.

Citation list. ISI Citation indexes, a resource to check up citations.

Compare. Look for similarities between ideas, theory or evidence.

Concept. A cognitive unit of meaning, an abstract representation of something.

Conclusion. The end point, often one defining statement.

Content aggregator. A company, such as EBSCO, which hosts a number of journals.

Contrast. Look for differences between ideas, theory or evidence.

Contribution. Adding something new to what is already known.

Copyright. The ownership of an idea, product or information. You must obtain permission to use it and cite it accurately.

Criticism. From the Greek word *kritikos*, meaning to judge. In this context, it is used to judge the work, not the person.

Critique. The argument, where you give your judgement, backed up with a discussion of the evidence, on the merit of ideas, theory, data or opinion or the truth of so-called 'facts'.

Debate. Argue from two or more viewpoints.

Define. Set out the precise meaning or use of a word or phrase.

Describe. Give a detailed account of something without critique.

Discuss. Examine by argument, giving reasons for and against.

Dissertation. An academic document, usually of a prescribed length.

Dumping. A sentence with one core idea, where several authors are cited in a list.

Effect size. In statistics, the magnitude of the effect of an independent variable on the dependent variable (magnitude of change in the dependent variable). In clinical research, the effect size is often the treatment effect.

Evaluate. Make an appraisal of the worth of something, often against pre-set criteria.

Evidence. The data (numerical or written narrative text) from which to develop a theory or argument. It is the proof.

Executive summary. Usually in a report, it presents the key findings, implications and recommendations.

Fact. A claim that needs to be verified. The notion that 'facts speak for themselves' is a weak argument; there has to be proof to back it up.

Forest plot. A graphical representation of the effect size and variation in multiple quantitative studies which each address the same question. A summary effect size and variability can also be represented on the same graph.

Funnel plot. A scatter plot of the treatment effect size relative to the study size. It is useful in identifying possible bias in meta-analysis.

Gantt chart. A time and task chart to plan and monitor progress on a project.

Grey literature. Documents written for a restricted audience, not formally published, that are outside the traditional collections and are thus less readily available.

Heterogeneous. Different: in statistical terms, data from more than one population. Not homogenous.

Homogenous. Same: in statistical terms, from one population.

Illustrate. Explain and make clear, often in a diagram or model.

Information Manager (or librarian). A person who works in a library, usually trained in information management.

Journal. An academic publication, usually on a specialised subject, which disseminates current research and thinking on a range of issues within the stated topic.

Justify. Explain or show adequate grounds for the decision or conclusion.

Keywords. A selection of subject-related words assigned to articles by authors and database compilers that allow searchers to identify existing work.

Library catalogue. An online index of all the materials in a library.

Literature review. A secondary-source, desk-based research method which critically describes and appraises a topic.

Literature search. A systematic and planned search of existing databases, textbooks and journals.

Mapping. Organising and relating the various elements and dimensions of knowledge in the topic, usually in a mind map.

Meta-analysis. A statistical technique to combine quantitative data from independent publications.

Methodology. An account of a research method associated within a research paradigm (positivist or interpretivist).

Narrative literature review. A research method which involves reviewing published and sometimes unpublished material. It usually begins with a rationale for the review. It consists of a narrative style.

Operationalise. To define variables and concepts so that they can be measured empirically and quantitatively.

Paradigm. Describes a cluster of beliefs which influences the manner in which members of a particular discipline study, in this case how research should be conducted and results reported or interpreted.

Peer review. The process of subjecting one's work to colleagues knowledgeable in the subject. It is usually done anonymously.

Plagiarism. To use someone else's ideas, words, sentences as if your own, without acknowledging their name.

Position. An opinion.

Preface. A statement by an author, or guest writer, at the beginning of the work that outlines its origins, purpose, scope and intended audience.

Primary data. Data generated by the researcher specifically for a project which did not previously exist.

Pro-forma. A template document on which to compile information in a standard way.

Quotation. The words of another author reproduced verbatim, in one's own work. Shorter quotations may be presented within quotation marks '…' whereas longer quotations (40 or more words) may be displayed as indented text.

Reasons. The contributing arguments which support your main argument or line of reasoning.

Reference list. A list of all sources cited in the text. The list is alphabetical if Harvard style, or numerical if Vancouver style.

Relevance. Having an appropriate or direct bearing on the matter in hand.

Re-view. Take a second look at something, examining it critically in detail.

Secondary data. Data previously collected for another purpose which may be reprocessed and re-analysed for a new project.

Sensitivity analysis. A repetitive re-analysis of data undertaken to identify the impact of different variables on the outcome of the analysis. Performed during a meta-analysis to confirm validity of findings.

Serendipity. Discovering something by chance.

Stringing. A sentence with one core idea, where several authors are cited in a list (*see also* dumping).

Synthesis. The combination of separate or diverse elements into a new coherent whole.

Systematic review. A review with a clearly stated purpose, a question, a defined search approach, stating inclusion and exclusion criteria, producing a qualitative appraisal of articles.

Textbook. A book written for students that provides current knowledge and theory of a given subject.

Theory. A set of explanatory principles, for example Darwin's Theory of Evolution.

Traditional narrative literature review (*see also* narrative review). A research method which involves reviewing published and unpublished material. It usually begins with a rationale for the review and is written in a narrative style.

Wiesel words. An informal term about vague words or words with an ambiguous meaning, giving the impression that something important is being said.

Zeitgeist. The specific attitudes of a particular time or period.

REFERENCES

Ackerman, L. (1997) Development, transition or transformation: the question of change in organisations. In Van Eynde, D. and Hoy, J. (eds), *Organization Development Classics*, San Francisco: Jossey-Bass.

American Psychological Association (2005) *Concise Rules of APA style*, Washington, DC: American Psychological Association.

Aveyard, H. (2007) *Doing a Literature Review in Health and Social Care*, Maidenhead: Open University Press.

Barkema, H.G. and Schijven, M. (2008) How do firms learn to make acquisitions? A review of past research and an agenda for the future, *Journal of Management*, 34: 594–634.

Bambra, C., Gibson, M., Sowden, A., Wright, K., Whitehead, M. and Petticrew, M. (2009) Tackling the wider social determinants of health inequalities: evidence from systematic reviews, *Journal of Epidemiology and Community Health* [online August 2009]. Accessed September 2009.

Barr, S. (2007) Factors influencing environmental attitudes and behaviours: a UK case study of household waste management, *Environment and Behaviour*, 39(4): 435–473.

Bereiter, C. (2002) *Education in Mind and the Knowledge Age*, Mahwah, NJ and London: Lawrence Erlbaum Associates.

Blumberg, B., Cooper, D.R. and Schindler, P.S. (2005) *Business Research Methods*, London: McGraw-Hill.

Bonnett, A. (2001) *How to Argue: A Student's Guide*, London: Prentice Hall/Pearson Education.

Brav, A., Graham, J.R., Harvey, C.H. and Michaely, R. (2005) Payout policy in the 21st century, *Journal of Financial Economics*, 77: 483–527.

Brignall, S. (1998) Financial performance measurement. In Innes, J. (ed.), *Handbook of Management Accounting*, London: GEE Publishing Limited.

Broadbent, M. (1999) *Measuring Business Performance*, London: Chartered Institute of Management Accountants.

Browne, M.N. and Keeley, S.M. (2004) *Asking the Right Questions: A Guide to Critical Thinking* (7th edn), Upper Saddle River, NJ; London: Pearson Prentice Hall.

Brownlie, D. (2007) Towards effective poster presentations: an annotated bibliography, *European Journal of Marketing*, 41(11/12): 1245–1283.

Bryman, A. (2004) *Social Research Methods* (2nd edn), Oxford: Oxford University Press.

Burnes, B. (1996) *Managing Change: A Strategic Approach to Organizational Dynamics* (2nd edn), London: Pitman.

Burtonwood, A., Hinchcliffe, A. and Tinkler, G. (1998) A prescription for quality: a role for the clinical pharmacist in general practice, *The Pharmaceutical Journal*, 261: 678–80.

Buzan, T. (2003) *The Mind Map Book*, London: BBC Books.

Ceglowski, D. and Bacigalupa, C. (2002) Keeping current in child care research: annotated bibliography – an update, *Early Childhood Research and Practice*, 4: 1. Open Access journals: www.doag.org. Accessed November 2009.

Christian, M.S., Bradley, J.C., Wallace, J.C. and Burke, M.J. (2009) Workplace safety: a meta-analysis of the roles of person and situation factors, *Journal of Applied Psychology*, 94(5): 1103–1127.

Collins, P.A. and Hayes, M.V. (2010) The role of urban municipal governments in reducing health inequalities: a meta-narrative mapping analysis, *Journal for Equity in Health*, 9(13). www.equityhealthj/com/contents/9/1/13. Accessed June 2010.

Cottrell, S. (2005) *Critical Reading Skills: Developing Effective Analysis and Argument*, Basingstoke: Macmillan.

Curran, C., Burchardt, T., Knapp, M., McDaid, D. and Li, B. (2007) Challenges in multi-disciplinary systematic reviewing: a study on social exclusion and mental health policy, *Social Policy and Administration*, 41(3): 289–312.

Currie, D. (2005) *Developing and Applying Study Skills*, London: Chartered Institute of Personnel and Development.

Davies, J., Foxall, G.R. and Pallister, J. (2002) Beyond the intention–behaviour mythology: an integrated model of recycling, *Marketing Theory*, 2(1): 29–113.

Davis, G., Phillips, P.S., Read, A.D. and Lida, Y. (2006) Demonstrating the need for the development of internal research capacity: understanding recycling participation using the Theory of Planned Behaviour in West Oxfordshire, UK, *Resources, Conservation and Recycling*, 46: 115–127.

De Cuyper, N., De Jong, J., De Witte, H., Isaksson, K., Rigotti, T. and Schalk, R. (2008) Literature review of theory and research on the psychological impact of temporary employment: towards a conceptual model, *International Journal of Management Review*, 10(1): 1–23.

DEFRA (Department of Environment, Food and Rural Affairs) (2007) *Waste and Resources Evidence Strategy for England 2007–11*. www.defra.gov.uk. Accessed July 2008.

Denzin, N.K. and Lincoln, Y.S. (2005) *The Sage Handbook of Qualitative Research*, London: Sage.

Department of Health (1999) *Saving Lives: Our Healthier Nation*, Cm 4386. London: HMSO.

Department of Health (2004) *Choosing Health: Making Healthy Choices Easier*, Cm 6374. London: HMSO.

Eggar, M., Smith, G.D., Schneider, M. and Minder, C. (1997) Bias in meta-analysis detected by a simple graphical test, *British Medical Journal*, 315: 629–634.

Elsevier (2008) *How to... write an abstract*, Oxford: Elsevier. www.info.emeraldinsight.com/authors. Accessed October 2008.

Essers, J. and Schreinemakers, J. (1997) Nonaka's subjectivist conception of knowledge in corporate knowledge management. *Knowledge Organization*, 24(1): 24–32.

Fergusson, D., Glass, K.C., Hutton, B. and Shapiro, S. (2005) Randomized controlled trials of Aprotonin in cardiac surgery: could clinical equipoise have stopped the bleeding? *Clinical Trials*, 2: 218–232.

Ferlie, E. (1997) Large-scale organisational and managerial change in health care: a review of the literature, *Journal of Health Services Research Policy*, 2(3): 180–188.

Furrer, O., Thomas, H. and Goussevskaia, A. (2008) The structure and evolution of the strategic management field: a content analysis of 26 years of strategic management research, *International Journal of Management Review*, 10(1): 25–51.

Gibaldi, J. (2003) *MLA Handbook for Writers of Research Papers*. New York: Modern Language Association of America.

Goldstein, R., Hulme, H. and Willits, J. (1997) Reviewing repeat prescribing – general practitioners and community pharmacists working together, *International Journal of Pharmacy Practice*, 6: 60–6.

Gourlay, S. (2006) Conceptualizing knowledge creation: a critique of Nonaka's theory, *Journal of Management Studies*, 43(7): 1415–1436.

Granas, A.G. and Bates, I. (1999) The effect of pharmaceutical review of repeat prescriptions in general practice, *International Journal of Pharmacy Practice*, 7: 264–275.

Greenhalgh, T. (2006) *How to Read a Paper: The Basis of Evidence-based Medicine*, BMJ Books. Oxford: Blackwell.

Grullon, G. and Michaely, R. (2002) Dividends, share repurchases, and the substitution hypothesis, *The Journal of Finance*, 52(40): 1649–1684.

GSR (2008) *Government Social Research Civil Service Rapid Evidence Assessment Toolkit*. www.gsr.gov.uk/professional_guidance/rea_toolkit/index. Accessed July 2008.

Hanlon, P. and Carlisle, S. (2008) Do we face a third revolution in human history? If so, how will public health respond? *Journal of Public Health*, 30(4): 355–361.

Hart, C. (1998) *Doing a Literature Review*, London: Sage.

Hartman, K.A. (2000) Studies of negative political advertising: an annotated bibliography, *Reference Services Review*, 28(3): 248–261.

Highways Agency (2009) Post-opening project evaluation: meta-analysis of Economic Impacts. www.bettertransport.org.uk/system/files/HA-POPE-economy.pdf. Accessed September 2009.

Hines, J.M., Hungerford, H.R. and Tomera, A.V. (1986) Analysis and synthesis of research on responsible environmental behaviour: a meta-analysis. *The Journal of Environmental Education*, 18(2): 1–8.

Hopkins, L. and Small, F. (2006) Antibiotic prophylaxis regimens and drugs for cesarean section (Cochrane Review), *The Reproductive Health Library*, 9. Oxford: Update Software Ltd. www.rhlibrary.com (reprinted from *The Cochrane Library*, Issue 1, 2006. Chichester: John Wiley & Sons). Accessed September 2009.

Hornik, J., Cherian, J., Madensky, M. and Narayana, C. (1995) Determinants of recycling behaviour: a synthesis of research results, *Journal of Socio-Economics*, 24(1): 105–27.

International Journal of Management Review, 10(1), March 2008.

Jankowitz, A.D. (2005) *Business Research Projects* (4th edn), London: Thompson.

Jensen, M.C. (1986) Agency costs of free cash flow, corporate finances, and takeovers, *The American Economic Review*, 76(29): 323–329. (Papers and Proceedings of the ninety eighth Annual Meeting of the American Economic Association.)

Jesson, J. and Lacey, F. (2006) How to do (or not to do) a critical literature review, *Pharmacy Education*, 6(2): 139–148.

Jesson, J. and Stone, I. (2008) *What Do We Currently Know about Barriers to Recycling Household Waste in the UK? A Literature Review*. Research Working Paper RP 0915. Birmingham: Aston Business School. www.abs.aston.ac.uk or www.m-e-l.co.uk. Accessed July 2009.

Johnson, R. and Clark, G. (2002) *Service Operations Management*, Harlow: Pearson Education.

Kahn, K.S., Kunz, R., Kleijnen, J. and Antes, G. (2003) *Systematic Reviews to Support Evidence Based Medicine*, London: Royal Society Medicine Press.

Karousakis, K. and Birol, E. (2008) Investigating household preference for kerbside recycling services in London: a choice experiment approach, *Journal of Environmental Management*, 88(4): 1099–1108.

Keith, N. and Frese, M. (2008) Effectiveness of error management training: a meta-analysis, *Journal of Applied Psychology*, 93(1): 59–69.

Kendall, G., Knust, S., Ribeiro, C.C. and Urrutia, S. (2009) Scheduling in sports: an annotated bibliography, *Computers and Operations Research*, 37(1): 1–19.

Kindig, D.A. (2007) Understanding health population terminology, *The Millbank Quarterly*, 85(1): 139–161.

Krska, J., Cromarty, J.A., Arris, F., Jamieson, D. and Hansford, D. (2000) Providing pharmaceutical care using a systematic approach, *Pharmacy Journal*, 265: 656–660.

Lee, M.P. (2008) A review of the theories of corporate social responsibility: its evolutionary path and the road ahead, *International Journal of Management Review*, 10(1): 53–73.

Lee, N. and Lings, I. (2008) *Doing Business Research*, London: Sage.

Levin, P. (2004) *Write Good Essays*, Maidenhead: Open University Press.

Lewin, K. (1958) Group decisions and social change. In Swanson, G.E., Newcomb, T.M. and Hartley, E.L. (eds), *Readings in Social Psychology*, New York: Holt, Rhinehart and Winston.

Lewis, S. and Clarke, M. (2001) Forest plots: trying to see the wood from the trees, *British Medical Journal,* 322: 1479–1480.

McDonald, S. and Oates, C. (2003) Reasons for non-participation in a kerbside recycling scheme, *Resources, Conservation and Recycling*, 39: 369–385.

Macinko, J.A. and Starfield, B. (2002) Annotated bibliography on equity in health, 1980–2001, *International Journal for Equity in Health*, 1(1): 1–20. www.equityhealthj.com/content/1/1/1. Accessed June 2003.

Mackie, C.A., Lawson, D.H., Campbell, A., Maclaren, A.G. and Waight, R.A. (1999) A ran-domised controlled trial of medication review in patients receiving polypharmacy in general practice, *Pharmacy Journal*, 265: R7.

Magenta Book (2005) Systematic Reviews for Policy Evaluation, *Magenta Book* Chapter 2. Guidance notes for policy evaluation and analysis. Background paper 2: what do we already know? Harnessing existing research. www.nationalschool.gov.uk/policyhub/evaluating_policy/magenta_book. Accessed August 2008.

Mak, W.S., Poon, C.Y.M., Pun, L.Y.K. and Cheung, S.F. (2007) Meta-analysis of stigma and mental health, *Social Science and Medicine*, 65: 245–261.

Martin, M., Williams, I.D., Clark, M. (2006) Social, cultural and structural influences on house-hold waste recycling: a case study, *Resources, Conservation and Recycling*, 42: 1–26.

Mays, N., Pope, C. and Popay, J. (2005) Systematically reviewing qualitative and quantitative evidence to inform management and policy making in the health field, *Journal of Health Services Research Policy*, 10(Supplement 1): 6–20.

Metcalfe, M. (2003) Author(ity): the literature review as expert witness, *Forum: Qualitative Social Research*, (4)1. www.qualitative-research.net/fqs/. Accessed April 2010.

Michaely, R.,Thaler, R.H. and Womack, K.L. (1995) Price reactions to dividend initiations and omissions: overreaction or drift, *The Journal of Finance*, 2(2): 573–608.

Miller, M.H. and Modigliani, F. (1961) Dividend policy, growth and the valuation of shares, *The Journal of Business*, 34(4): 441–433.

Miller, R.L. and Brewer, J.D. (2003) *The A–Z of Social Research*, London: Sage.

Murch, S.H., Anthony, A. and Casson, D.H. et al. (2004) Retraction of an interpretation, *Lancet*, 36: 750.

Neville, C. (2010) *The Complete Guide to Referencing and Avoiding Plagiarism*, 2nd edn, Maidenhead: Open University Press.

NPC (National Prescribing Centre) and NHSE (1998) *Prescribing Support: A Resource Document and Guide for the New NHS*, Liverpool: National Prescribing Centre.

Oates, C.J. and McDonald, S. (2006) Recycling and the domestic division of labour: is green pink or blue? *Sociology*, 40(3): 417–433.

Ogilvie, D., Egan, M., Hamilton, V. and Pettigrew, M. (2005) Systematic reviews of health effects of social interventions: 2. Best available evidence: how low should you go? *Journal of Epidemiology and Community Health*, 59: 886–892.

Olin and Uris libraries (2008) *How To Prepare an Annotated Bibliography*, New York: Cornell University library. www.library.cornell.edu/olinuris. Accessed October 2008.

O'Neill, J. (2005) Reviewing the literature. In Wellington, J., Bathmaker, A., Hunt, C., McCullock, G. and Sikes, P. (eds), *Succeeding with Your Doctorate*, London: Sage, pp. 72–91.

Pang, F., Drummond, M. and Song, F. (1999) *The Use of Meta-analysis in Economic Evaluation* (Discussion paper 173), York: Centre for Health Economics.

Pearce, F. (2010) Censorship or high standards: how scientists kept sceptics out of print, *The Guardian*, 3 February: 12–13.

Pears, S.R. and Shields, G. (2008) *Cite Them Right: The Essential Referencing Guide*, Newcastle upon Tyne: Pear Tree Books.

Perrin, D. and Barton, J. (2001) Issues associated with transforming household attitudes and opinions into material recovery: a review of two kerbside recycling schemes, *Resources, Conservation and Recycling*, 33: 61–74.

Petticrew, M. and Roberts, H. (2006) *Systematic Reviews in the Social Sciences: A Practical Guide*, Oxford: Blackwell.

Pilbean, C. and Denyer, D. (2007) *Teaching Systematic Reviewing of Literature Workshop*, Cranfield University AIM training materials.

Plos Medicine Editors (2006) The impact factor game, *Plos Med*, 3(6): e291. www.medicine. plosjournals.org. Accessed February 2009.

Plos Medicine Editors (2007) Peer review in Plos Medicine, *Plos Med*, 4(1): e58. www.medicine. plosjournals.org. Accessed February 2009.

RevMan (2008) Review Manager (RevMan) [Computer program]. Version 5.0. Copenhagen: The Nordic Cochrane Centre, The Cochrane Collaboration.

Ridley, D. (2008) *The Literature Review: A Step-by-step Guide for Students*, London: Sage.

Robinson, G.M. and Read, A.D. (2005) Recycling behaviour in a London Borough: results from large-scale household surveys, *Resources, Conservation and Recycling*, 45: 70–83.

Shacklady-Smith, A. (2006) Appreciating the challenge of change. In Walshe, K. and Smith, J. (eds), *Healthcare Management*, Maidenhead: Open University Press, pp. 381–398.

Shaw, P.J., Lyas, J.K., Maynard, S.J. and van Vugt, M. (2007) On the relationship between set-out rates and participation ratios as a tool for enhancement of kerbside household waste recycling, *Journal of Environmental Management*, 83: 34–43.

Smallbone, T. (2005) How can domestic households become part of the solution to England's recycling problems? *Business Strategy and the Environment*, 14: 110–122.

Smith, K.E., Fooks, G., Collin, J., Weishaar, H. and Gilomore, A.B. (2010) Is the increasing policy use of Impact Assessment in Europe likely to undermine efforts to achieve healthy public policy? *Journal of Epidemiological Community Health*, 64: 478–487. Online version. Accessed June 2010.

Souza, J.P., Pileggi, C. and Cecatti, J.G. (2007) Assessment of funnel plot symmetry and publication bias in reproductive health meta-analyses: an analytical survey, *Reproductive Health*, 4(1): 3.

Srivastava, S.K. (2007) Green supply-chain management: a state-of-the-art literature review, *International Journal of Management Review*, 9(1): 53–80.

Sutton, A.J., Duval, S.J., Tweedie, R.L., Abrams, K.R. and Jones, D.R. (2000) Empirical assessment of effect of publication bias on meta-analyses, *British Medical Journal*, 320: 1574–1577.

Swain, H. (2009) How to be a student No 61: the art of learning how to think, *Education Guardian*, 10 March: 12.

Sweet, M. and Moynihan, R. (2007) Improving population health: the uses of systematic review, New York: Millbank Memorial Fund. www.milbanj.org. Accessed January 2008.

Sykes, W., Westwood, P. and Gillingham, J. (1996) Development of a review programme for repeat prescription medicines, *Pharmacy Journal*, 256: 458–460.

Thomas, C., Yoxon, M., Slater, R. and Leaman, J. (2004) Changing recycling behaviour: an evaluation of attitudes and behaviour to recycling in western riverside areas of London, Waste 2004 Conference. Stratford-upon-Avon. Accessed September 2008.

Tong, A., Sainsbury, P. and Craig, J. (2007) Consolidated criteria for reporting qualitative research (COREQ): a 32-item checklist for interviews and focus groups, *International Journal for Quality in Health Care*, 19(6): 349–357.

Torgerson, C. (2003) *Systematic Reviews*, London: Continuum.

Tranfield, D., Denyer, D. and Smart, P. (2003) Towards a methodology for developing evidence-informed management knowledge by means of systematic review, *British Journal of Management*, 14: 207–222.

Tuch, C. and O'Sullivan, N. (2007) The impact of acquisitions on firm performance: a review of the evidence, *International Journal of Management Reviews*, 9(2): 141–170.

Tucker, P. and Spiers, D. (2003) Attitudes and behaviour change in household waste management behaviours, *Journal of Environmental Planning and Management*, 46(2): 289–307.

Turrini, A., Cristofoli, D., Frosini, F. and Nasi, G. (2010) Networking literature about determinants of network effectiveness, *Public Administration*, 88(2): 528–550.

Wade, C.A., Turner, H.M., Rothstein, H.R. and Lavenburg, J.G. (2006) Information retrieval and the role of the information specialist in producing high-quality sytematic reviews in the social, behavioural and educational sciences, *Evidence and Policy*, 2(91): 89–108.

Whiting, E. (1986) *A Guide to Business Performance*, London: Macmillan.

Williams, I.D. and Kelly, J. (2003) Green waste collection and the public's recycling behaviour in the Borough of Wyre, England, *Resources, Conservation and Recycling*, 38: 139–159.

Wilson, K.A. and Jesson, J. (2003) Dispensing activity in a community pharmacy-based repeat dispensing pilot project, *International Journal of Pharmacy Practice*, 11: 225–232.

Zermansky, A.G., Petty, D.R., Raynor, D.K., Freemantle, Vail, N. and Lowe, C.J. (2001) Randomized controlled trial of clinical medication review by a pharmacist of elderly patients receiving repeat prescriptions in general practice, *British Medical Journal*, 323: 1340–1343.

INDEX